CW01424558

# **polari** plays

Published by Polari Plays, an imprint of Polari Press.

polari.com  @polaripress

ISBN: 978-1-914237-28-7

First published in the UK in 2024.

Copyright © Rik Barnett, 2024 under exclusive licence to Polari Press Ltd. Rik Barnett have asserted their right under the Copyright, Designs and Patents Act, 1988, to be identified as authors of this work.

Cover design and typesetting by Peter Collins for Polari. Typeset in a custom typeface by Bijou Type and Roslindale by David Jonathan Ross. Printed on responsibly sourced paper using vegetable inks. Polari Press is committed to reducing its environmental impact.

Polari Press does not have any control over, or responsibility for, any third-party websites referred to in this book. All internet addresses given in this book were correct at the time of going to press. The authors and publisher regret any inconvenience caused if addresses have changed or sites have ceased to exist, but can accept no responsibility for any such changes.

All rights whatsoever in this play are strictly reserved and application for performance etc should be made before rehearsals by emailing contact@polari.press. All professional/amateur production enquiries should be made to them. Permission must be sought whether the title is presented for charity or gain and whether or not admission is charged. No alterations to the text or title are permitted without the authors' prior written consent. Both Polari Press and the playwright welcome applications for amateur productions and public readings.

No part of this book may be reproduced, stored in a retrieval system, or transmitted in any form, by any means, not known or yet to be invented, including mechanical, electronic, photocopying, recording, videotaping, or otherwise, without the prior written permission of the publisher.

A catalogue record for this book is available from the British Library.

To find out more about our authors and work, visit polari.press and sign up to our newsletter.

# rik barnett

# bosie

---

This version was first performed at the Fitzgerald, Manchester, 10 July 2023.

*Written and performed by* Rik Barnett
*Directed by* Tuirenn Hurstfield
*Produced by* Northern Rep

# Bosie

by Rik Barnett

## Characters

**BOSIE** *Male, 25 years old*

## Setting

*Act One: Room at the Hotel Des Deux Mondes*
*22 Avenue de L'Opera, Paris*

*Act Two: Room at the Hotel Des Deux Mondes*
*22 Avenue de L'Opera, Paris*

## Time

*Act One: Tuesday, 7th May 1895. Late afternoon.*
*Oscar has been released on £5,000 bail.*

*Act Two: Wednesday, 29th May 1895. Early evening.*
*Oscar was sentenced to two years hard labour four days ago.*

## Content warning

*Derogatory language towards sex workers, women and Black men. Mention of suicide. Strong language and sexual themes throughout, including discussion of sex with a fourteen-year-old boy.*

# Act One

*A room in the Hotel Des Deux Mondes, 22 Avenue de L'Opera, Paris. There is a tea-tray on the bed.* **BOSIE** *enters, removes his outerwear then touches the teacup.*

**BOSIE**     They didn't even warm the cup!

How the hell did this happen?
I'm a lord for fuck's sake!

*Beat.*

Lord Alfred! Lord Alfred Bruce Douglas!
I'm Bosie.
An I'm a star, in one way or another.

Even my friends call me Bosie. What friends?
I suppose that is what I shall be known as, BOSIE –
Oscar's Bosie!
It's all about HIM! It's what everyone wants to know about...
Oscar.
*(Unenthusiastically)* Oscar and me? Where we went?
What we wore? What we did!
That's what they...

I am a wonderful, charming companion.

Oscar loves me, adores me, thinks of me in countless ways... and I love him, in my own "little way".

As I told my mother... I am passionately fond of Oscar.

He is the reason I am in this situation.

At least I've got some notoriety from it all, my name in the papers, mention of my work!

I am going to be blunt about things.
People will promise you the world, and yet you end up... exiled to France.

An outcast.

It's my father's fault actually.
ALL of THIS: My being here; Oscar in prison.

BOSIE *begins to empty his luggage, a letter falls out.*

All dear Papa wants is for me to be back in the fold.
He has always sent the most desperate letters.
Promises me the world, as long as I follow his terms and conditions...

It's always his way or no way... he wrote this saying that
he will "send me money" and "give me an allowance"
stating that "I should go and visit the South Sea Islands
for a while as there are many beautiful girls there".
It's such an obscene request... the only catch to it all,
I must NEVER see Oscar again... NO!

My father. I hate him!

He has a face like a bowl of old oats and a personality
to match.
Thankfully I didn't inherit either.
The "relationship" I have with my father... putting it
simply. Putting it kindly. I don't like the man. "Despise"
is a word that springs to mind.
My father, the Marquis of Queensbery. John.
No need to bother with all of his silly fanciful titles.

He was made into a lieutenant at the age of fifteen when
he was in the navy, at the same time he came into his
inheritance, I believe all that just made him power mad.

Well, THAT and the madness that stampedes through
HIS family.

The way he would speak to us; he'd just explode over

nothing, over trivial little things like a scuff on your shoe
or the pillow on your bed not being "straight".

BOSIE *messes up the pillows on the bed.*

We should have realised back then that he was a dick.
Ever the winner.

BOSIE *claps sarcastically.*

Well done DADDY!

He wins once more. After all, I'm the one in exile.
And him... I'm sure he is sitting happy with his whores,
drinking and smoking to excess like some decrepit
beast.

Everyone who knows of me, is aware of my upset. My
fucking hatred. It's all HIS fault. Some father... doesn't
even deserve THAT title.

It astounds me—still to this day—of what it was that
my mother actually saw in him, for I see NO redeeming
qualities... other than his bank account.
From which I have redeemed often!
But I won't have access to such things now.
Not until I visit those whores on the South Sea Islands!

I asked mother, once, why she was with him?
She said in a flurry of worry "what if he were to hear?"

I shrugged.

"It would upset him dearly, you don't want to ever upset
anyone my dear, dear Bosie".

Aww, bless Mummy.

I don't agree and I suppose that makes me a bad person.
Some people deserve to suffer!
I could reel off a list of several people right now if I had to.

It really is the hatred that I have for Father that led to
Oscar's downfall.

Daddy's intolerance. Daddy's stupidity.

**BOSIE** *gets his box of letters, he adds the letter to the box
and looks through the others.*

He would write such utterly disgusting things to me.
Continually threatening to disown me, stop all my
money, be cruel and demeaning.

**BOSIE** *opens and reads a letter.*

"Never in my experience have I seen such a sight as that
in your horrible features."

*He laughs.*

I sent him a wire in response to this. One line, I said,
"what a funny little man you are".


He must have been absolutely seething, in his response
back he said that he'd give me the "thrashing of my life"
as well as "cut off my money"...
I do HATE the way he makes financial threats.
Nothing upsets me more in life, and he has always
known it.
But, to agitate him more, I had my lawyer send him a
letter stating that I am willing to forfeit my allowance
for my eternal friendship with Oscar.


And I did.


No more money from Daddy!


Thankfully Mother and Grandfather gave me extra.
They provided me with the ability to live the way I have
always been inclined. Oscar also helped; always ready to
buy dinner. Pay for my desires.

**BOSIE** *closes the box.*

> I wish it were Daddy in prison. I'd do anything to have it
> be that way.

> I'd sell my soul. What's left of it.

*Beat.*

> As a child, my legs were not quite right. It got to the
> point that mother had to take me to the doctor.
> It turned out that I had knocked knees.

> I had to wear an iron brace.

> My father was absolutely disgusted.

> The first time he saw me in the back brace, he was
> utterly repulsed.
> He refused to acknowledge me. I was a nine-year-old child.
> HIS nine-year-old child!
> It was so painful; it felt like my own father had cast me
> out, for something completely out of my control.

> Still, even with the back brace, mother—the darling—
> would continually tell me how exquisitely beautiful I was.
> I love her so.

I am thankful that my mother was there, as she always is.
But then, she isn't here now, is she?
The cunt.

They are so off, Mother and Father! Chalk and cheese.
Especially when it came to raising us children. As a
boy they made my views towards certain things rather
muddied.

Religion, for instance. You see, Father is an assertive
atheist, but then Mother would take us to church on a
Sunday. I never really knew what to believe.

It's become clear as an adult... Start the day with a
prayer and end it with an orgy. Something to be said for
Sodom and Gomorrah.

My mother raised me on the dry bones of a dull religion.

We should live our life for the here and now rather than
fretting about what will happen when we are dead and
what "judgement" we may face.
Because after all, we'll be dead, won't we?

I feel sorry for Mother, and the rest.
Imagine being so persuaded into believing in a god and

the purity of it all, the notion that you WILL be saved in
this life and the next... Utter bullshit!

If God is "ever-loving", he'll accept me.
But Hell, well... must be filled with the most exciting
and fun individuals, the prince of Hell and Charles the
Second... Now that's an orgy.

My view on the monarchy drastically changed too. I used
to think of it as being so wonderful and well... "golden".
Mother is the biggest champion of the royals. "Ra, ra, ra."

Now I think that Queen Victoria is an absolute
heathen. She leaves the dykes alone but persecutes
the homosexuals. You know it takes a "peculiar" type
of woman to do such a thing. Most of her government
should be locked up! I've seen enough of them with
renters at one time or another. It's ludicrous!
I wrote to her... asking for her help with Oscar.
"NO." I wasn't even given a personal response.
The pig!

I am one for thinking that leaders should be attractive.

Beauty represents a lot. It represents good stock,
strength, nobility.

Something went VERY wrong through the timeline of
our English monarchy, that's for sure. Maybe it was all
that inbreeding; either way, we've ended up with that
royal, gnarly shrew.

Between you and me, I think we should do away with the
monarchy altogether.

They're nothing but trouble.

But I do hear that little Queenie serves the most
delicious chocolates at her garden parties. Simply
stupendous. So, on second thought, perhaps we should
do away with the monarchy but keep their parties! I do
love to mix with the elite.

My grandfather is the one who opened the royal doors
for me.

He introduced me to the Prince of Wales. The Prince
always made quite a fuss over me whenever we met...
what a charming gentleman HE is, unlike the rest.

There was one dinner that Grandfather threw at the
Travellers' Club. I was sat across from the Duke of
Cambridge who only went and nodded off to sleep.

So impertinent.

I "spilt" my wine in the Duke's direction.

He soon woke up.

Royals – they think they are SO above it all.

I think that what they do in the Americas is rather a splendid idea. There, they elect people to power, unlike us electing our puppets.

When I was younger, Mother said that she and I would perhaps travel and see America one day, together, just the two of us.

Mother found a replacement for my father, someone else to give all her love to... Me.

My parents' marriage disintegrated, for good reason.

Father took a mistress, a whore named Ellen who had a reputation and history with which no one wants association. Mother divulged how Father suggested a ménage à trois and them all live together.

How scandalous.

Mother was forced to file for a divorce; court
proceedings took less than fifteen minutes.

Mother is all about keeping up appearances.
She always has been.
She was uneasy with my "friendship". A man nearing his
forties and an undergraduate. Shock. Shock. Horror.
Our friendship was being adversely discussed by her
social circles. A member of her bridge club had asked
with an arched eyebrow about my "friend" and poor
Mother was flummoxed.

It is positively monstrous the way people talk about you
behind your back, about things that are entirely true.

But poor Mother had already suffered such scandal in
her life and worked so hard to keep her social grounding.

She had words with Oscar, took him for a walk in the
garden while he was staying with us in Bracknell.
She warned him of my extreme vanity, my need for
extravagance, lack of money sense, my temper.

Didn't falter Oscar.
He was already WELL AWARE of those traits of mine,
and many others.

Oh, but my temper – my temper and tantrums kill him
and "wreck the loveliness of life", but I just write and beg
for forgiveness and Oscar being Oscar ALWAYS forgives
me. His love for me will always triumph over any silly,
petty squabble.

And let's face it, I do come from an extremely theatrical
family, so my heightened nature should always be taken
with a pinch of salt.


There was a moment that Oscar was worried about me
deeply. He'd had enough of my hysterics and lack of
interest in anything academic.

Who wants to read a book when I can fuck a boy?


So, Oscar and mother collaborated and came up with an
enticing offer.


Mother's close childhood friend Ethel—a woman who
is always doused in the most exquisite diamonds, but
still never enough to distract from her ghastly crooked
smile—well, she had married Sir Evelyn, a diplomatic
agent in Egypt. Spending time with him makes reading
the dictionary sound like a fun activity.


They invited me—with my mother's overbearing
influence—to come and stay with them at the agency in

Cairo for some months.

Oscar said we should remain apart for at least two or
three years.
That killed me.

The few weeks before I left for Egypt there was a shift.
A coldness.
It was like we had become bored of one another.
He would talk and I wouldn't listen, he would hold me
and I would pull away.
Oscar became very into his renters.
They seemed to occupy his time.

I was off to Egypt.
He can have his renters, what with their superior wit
and intelligence.
They only listen to him because they are being PAID to.

I left for Egypt.

It's swarming with English men and women, what with
the archaeological glories and monuments. Those of
which I find to be so very garish and unattractive.
Dog-headed men?

I say, slap a plaque on it and move it into the British Museum and let's just have done with it.

I met two young queers, Benson and Hitchens.

Benson—a boy whose skin goes the most repulsive red in strong sunshine—Well he's the third son of the Archbishop of Canterbury.
He tried to convince me that "dark meat" is more delicious.
No.
They are all too... dominating. Not for me.
That's my role.

Hitchens—a boy whose disgustingly receding hairline makes it perfectly acceptable to wear a hat at all times—
He's a writer... a rather desperate one at that.
Desperate to be published.

We were all friends: loving life, talking, sharing... I told them everything about Oscar. Even had Hitchens meet him, upon his return to England.
Hitchens acquired everything he needed, and so wrote his 'book'.

*The Green Carnation*. It's a scandalous read.
Odious in fact.

Thankfully, due to the trial it's been withdrawn from sale. A small bonus of all of this, I suppose.

Such mediocre drivel.

I was in Egypt for three months.
While there, family and friends tried to fob off some position to me in Constantinople.
That was NEVER going to happen.

But in all that time, I didn't hear from Oscar. Not once.
His silence was torture.
I had written and telegraphed countless times.
But nothing in return, that is until I got one telegram, one dirty, thoughtless telegram saying, "it is best that we do not contact each other".

FUCK!

I left Cairo and headed straight to Paris. I sent Oscar copious telegrams begging him to meet me there. But when I arrived at my hotel there was only a letter waiting for me… saying that a meeting was "out of the question".

What am I without Oscar? I have nothing without him.

I put every thought and feeling into a telegram, it must have been ten or eleven pages long.

I had BEGGED Oscar to come, normally that would have worked.
So, I added some of that dramatic flair... I told him that my life wouldn't be worth living without him in it!
That it would be easy for me to lay sleeping for eternity dreaming of him rather than living a life without him.

Oscar is well aware of my family's tendency towards suicide.

So... he hurried to me!

When I saw him, he was so smartly dressed and I saw such deep adoration in his eyes.
I clutched his hand with all my might.
With him by my side I was home.
It's like I'm safe. I'm important when I'm with him.
We spent the night at my hotel... by the morning he had more than agreed to renew our friendship.

Returning with him, to London, I was still clutching his hand at every available opportunity.

We got back into the swing of life, the dinners,
the laughter, the fun, and the renters.

Oh, those renters!

*Beat.*

Father likes his renters too, except his have tits.

He would write to mother in explicit detail about
his exploits.
He played everyone around him in the most disgusting
way – all for his own sordid amusement.

My eldest brother, Francis, a wonderful young man.
Always so happy and full of life. So joyous.

When it was just Francis and me, we would talk
candidly. About the world, politics, god, love... MEN.
Everything!

He told me once when we were both a lot younger that
"we are all beasts and nothing more".

I often think of that.

That we are all just savages.

We're wild animals in top hats and petticoats.
Pretending, always pretending.

Francis and I talked of love, true, real love.
Which is where? Can I ask? Hmm?

But my brother ended up finding it.

Just before I started to board at Winchester, Francis
said to me, "enjoy every moment, do everything and
anything you want to do! It's freedom, real freedom!"
He then put his head on a tilt of an angle and said,
"Enjoy all the experiences on offer, Bosie!"

I hadn't a clue what he was talking about, "freedom"
and…

BOSIE *angles his head.*

"Experiences"… but I think it took all of what?…
Forty-eight hours before I "found out".

I know Francis had had the most wonderful time
boarding at Harrow, most "boys like us" often do.
He got into Lord Rosebery there; they were the best
of "friends".

Francis would tell me about their trips to the lake.
How their conversations were just utterly deep,
truthful and intimate.
Meaningful.
Rosebery married young, a woman whom my brother
referred to as "homely".

The wife, thankfully, died in '90, so a brief marriage. But
her passing made my brother and Rosebery even closer.

My brother had never been bright or interested in
politics or diplomacy... so it did seem "strange" when
Rosebery got a seat in the House of Commons and
Francis was made into his "private secretary".

They spent all their time together.

They were so in love.

Francis wrote me saying how incredibly happy he was.
Simple bliss.
I do wonder what that must feel like.

My brother was treated so well by Rosebery.
Francis even got a seat in the House of Lords. The sort
of thing one wants access to in one's own family.

Father was jealous of Francis.

Understandably, because he lost HIS seat in the House
of Lords due to his adamant atheism.

One must declare belief in God to have a political say...
Madness.

Then, last March, Rosebery became prime minister.

Francis had told me that father spoke with Rosebery
privately and threatened him! He wanted his help to
vigorously prosecute Oscar and if he didn't then he
was going to expose Rosebery's homosexuality to the
government.

Francis said that he couldn't stand by and watch
Rosebery's life get consumed and destroyed by Father.

So my brother distanced himself from Oscar and me,
he didn't want any more upset from association.

Father wrote to Queen Victoria, informing her that
Rosebery was a bad influence on his sons.

Then the rumour mill about my brother and Rosebery
really started to heat up.

That's what influenced my brother's proposal to Miss Ellis... I'll never be seen dead doing such a thing.

But what Francis had said to me about "standing by and seeing Rosebery's life get destroyed" played so strongly in my mind when I received the news.

Last October, the eighteenth.
My brother was out hunting.

He had lost his fallen bird and took his shotgun into the hedge by the woods to retrieve it.

It was our father's fault... it was.
I know it and HE knows it. It's just another reason why I despise him.

My father still had the audacity to write me a week or so later saying that the blame for my brother's suicide—or "accident" as he put it—lay with Rosebery. That—and I quote—

**BOSIE** *recites from memory.*

"Snob queers like Rosebery have corrupted not just Francis but you as well."

He is a pathetic human being. His son, my brother.
Where is his fucking heart?

It was made out to the public and published that Francis
had died from a "hunting accident"...

The doctor's report stated that the charge entered his
mouth, fracturing his lower jaw and passing through the
roof of his mouth.
Death said to be instantaneous.
The "ACCIDENTAL" death that is.
It's all SUCH a farce!

I miss my brother.
I miss my mother.
Oscar.

*Beat.*

It was Lionel, my good friend Lionel Johnson, who
introduced me to Oscar. Lionel believed that Oscar and
I were "made for one another". Lionel said that I was
"the most beautiful young man alive and a fine poet".
He said we'd adore one another.

He arranged our visit to Oscar's house on Tite Street.
It was summer, in the afternoon.

I was perspiring a little from the heat.

A month shy of my twenty-first birthday.

Oscar was thirty-seven.

Lionel and I got there in a Hansom, he always loved the hard thrust back when riding over cobbles.

We were shown into Oscar's book-lined study and he made his entrance.

He wasn't like the company I usually keep, certainly not how one would be greeted.

Kisses and tactile affection.

As soon as he began to talk I was utterly impressed and well... mesmerised by him.

Now at first glance—I'll be honest—I thought Oscar to be a rather unprepossessing looking gentleman.

Rather regal in a way.

Oscar later told me that he thought I acted coy upon our first meeting, yet he could see a great fire in my eyes.

He said that he wanted to discover that fire... and, he did! Oh, like so many others, he most certainly did.

Before I left that first meeting, I was led upstairs to meet Oscar's wife, Constance.

I "liked" her very much.

A sweet woman, a little dull but sweet. A good mother.

Two boys.
I didn't like them either; children, HIS children with
THAT woman. They should be placed in the nursery with
the door firmly closed.
It drove me mad when Oscar would insist on visiting
them. If he did so, he was wise to return to me with a
gift. Sadly, as time went on, Constance became distant,
cold and well, rather slanderous.

She always knew.

In time Robbie Ross and other such "friends" polluted
her against me fully.

Oscar invited me to dine with him at the Albermarle Club.
I leapt at the chance of a second meeting.

We sat at the corner table, it was a particularly busy
night. Oscar sat next to me.
Closer than what would be considered "appropriate".
As the waiter took our order, he discreetly and gently
put his hand on my thigh and delicately squeezed.

My God.

Such advances excited me.

I was foolish and I was swept away – and that is
EXACTLY what I wanted!

I was in the centre of the most exhilarating spider's web
and "YES", I was more than happy to 'play' the part of
the prey.
But little did Oscar know how I was the hunter as much
as I played the part of the hunted.

At the Albemarle Club, Oscar gave me an inscribed copy
of *Dorian Gray*.

I took it back to Oxford with me.
It's one of my prized possessions.

It really was the beginning of a wonderful relationship…
Now the first few months of our friendship remained
chaste.
I loved spending time with him, seeing him talk and
tell his stories would fill me with glee and the way he
would look at me filled me with warmth like I have
never felt before.

Also, he would treat me, you know, to tea at Café Royal,
to a silk scarf, to whatever I wanted.

He was wonderful!
It was wonderful!

While I was an undergraduate at Oxford, he would visit me.

After I had seen him over and over, there was one
afternoon Oscar asked me to pay for our lunch.
This wouldn't do.
I had to make myself the most important person in
Oscar's life.
So, I did... give in to him.

And for the record, I did with him and allowed him to
do to me just what was done among boys at Winchester
and Oxford and...

**BOSIE** *wafts his hand etc. etc.*

...and you know the rest.

Standard schoolboys' practice.

Oscar eventually realised that I was being "physical" with
him in order to please him; I felt like I owed it to him...

To be blunt, I did it in exchange for dinner with Oscar's
publisher Ward Lock and Company.

I write, that's all I know how to do. Well... that and fuck.

Oscar actually fucked one of the young clerks who
worked there.

As a writer, Oscar's fortunes really rose with the success
of *No Importance*. He was able to grow more expensive in
his tastes and appearance, especially when it came to me.
Money was pouring in from his shows and invitations
were pouring in from the aristocracy.
The whole social and artistic world of bloody London
was infected by the dialogue of his plays.
Oscar's name was in everyone's mouth.

He had achieved what I have ALWAYS wanted.

I was happy for him. For us.
I returned from Oxford, without a degree.
I didn't care.

I was living a wild, bohemian, beautiful lifestyle.
A lifestyle that would make the world jealous.

We would make our entrance, and everyone would look.
Such attention.
Made me feel so special. So important.
I deserve to be looked at.

*Beat.*

That summer, Oscar took a cottage in Goring. I joined him.


He had to take a servant, so I decided that we take the
ugliest one available.
There was a beautiful young man from Shrewsbury,
he had a small frame, blue eyes... simply perfect.
But I didn't want the competition.
Our servant boy had the most horrendous complexion
and the most peculiar pear-shaped body for one of the
male sex.


In Goring, Oscar and I had a joyful time together, to
begin with... Basking in the sun, swimming in the
river, entertaining guests, reading, writing... Perhaps
a little too much writing on Oscar's part, which led to
one horrendous argument. Oscar had been working,
I suddenly never saw him. What was the point in our
being there together? I was practically ignored.

I saw more of him in London.
So, I demanded we return there and he complained at
the expense of it all.

He is so CHEAP.

Oscar has spent a fortune on me; and I'm sure he has
kept every tab, tally and bill.

HE chose to entertain my expensive, luxurious tastes...
shame on him if he had to account for each and every
penny – pathetic.

A real gentleman shouldn't have to worry or even think
what is in his bank account.

We had the argument, at the cottage, it was when the
Hets were visiting.
The Hets, so blissfully unaware. They know that he
dotes on me.
The Homs, they were always in on the game.

But this argument, it was embarrassing. Such a scene
he caused, the Hets witnessing a lovers tiff... so much
for the friendship façade.

Oscar refused my request to leave and I launched the
inkwell off his desk right across the room.
Well, I just knocked it over his crisp white shirt and
latest pages.

I ended up going back to London alone.
But I did return to our little cottage three short days later.
I always get the nicest gifts after our little fights.

He reinforced bad habits. Scream loud enough and
you'll get it. Hit hard enough and you'll get it. Fuck well
enough, you'll get it.
Oscar never put my habits into practice for himself... so
I was forced to make up for that for the both of us.

But, something strange about being with someone you
love a hundred per cent of the time. It's not natural.
It drives you crazy.

By the end of our time together at the cottage, we were
both rather tired, and in need of some "alone time",
some freedom.
Oscar went to Dinard for a fortnight and I went and
stayed with my Uncle George.

I do love Oscar. He helped me grow.

He taught me so much. That any man has the potential
to be splendid.
To not scoff at mysteries one does not understand.
To not doubt a possibility of a "god". That I should keep
a clear head in judgement of things. To judge things only
on their essential points.

Not that I implement these lessons with much
regularity... they are still invaluable.

He was always trying to teach me something; that I
should put in the time, the value of sitting down and
writing solidly, to WORK!
But what a waste of a young person's life!
Perhaps things would be different for me if I had just
listened.

People light up when they see Oscar enter a room. It's like
they instantly see his innate talent and wonderment.

Oscar wanted me to have that; he would say if I just keep my
focus and prose going I would be as successful as I want...

He believed in me. Not many others did with as much
passion as Oscar. But he was always passionate about
me; maybe his passions for my poetry were a spillover

from his passions for my body.
Either way it was there.

Now no one can help or control where one's passions lie…

My instincts and desires are drawn less towards men—
old men especially—and more towards younger boys.
Oscar was very understanding; he was very amenable to
'open' fun. HE is married for fuck's sake…

But with regards to our open fun, Oscar was to never,
NEVER engage in sexual activity with Robbie Ross
EVER again.

Robbie, Robbie, Robbie…

Oscar and I have a mutual friend, Robbie, well; Oscar
knew him before me, and I would struggle to call him an
actual friend.

Robbie was Oscar's… you know.

*(Distastefully)* Little Robbie Ross.

Robbie has never stopped loving Oscar, because of that
I can never truly trust him.
He is the worst kind of quill swallower.

When I first met Robbie, I knew how strongly Oscar felt
about him and I hated it. Plus, he was a Canadian.

He was frightfully effeminate. With porcelain-white skin
and rat-like features.
I was half expecting him to curtsey.

I saw myself in him, in his fey effeminate ways...
It's everything I strive and fight so hard not to be.
I am a man.
Whereas he is a small, slight quim with considerable
charm of manner...
He plays up to those he wishes to impress, the ultimate
panderer. Another quality I hate!

He has perfected his chameleon-like skills to befriend
anyone and smoothly navigate around any upset.

Initially, I got to know Robbie, I found myself tolerating
him and at times even liking him, his character, his beliefs.

I will say that Robbie has more guts than most people
I know.
I give him credit for that.
Even though we all know the story of the King's College
boys hearing screams of a woman only to rush in to

discover little Robbie Ross perched atop a chair with
a mouse at his feet. Wailing like a woman in birth,
so the tales go.
Terrible.

He ended up leaving his studies at King's College due
to the bullying he got for his effeminate nature and
mannerisms, which do make me want to savagely
attack him.

I digress. The reason why Robbie has so much guts isn't
anything to do with actual vermin but rather that after
he left his studies, Robbie gathered all of his family
together and confessed to them all that... he was a
homosexual. Just like that. It's an incredibly brave move
and one I shall not be following in.

He works. He's a critic. He's no Oscar Wilde. No one's
a writer like MY Oscar. But Robbie is very cutting.
You don't want to be on the wrong side of one of his reviews.
Believe me, I have been.

And I am sure I am right now, being judged and talked
about by him... the foul, self-righteous, little prick.
I'm happy that he and Constance were SO close. They
can revel in their jealousy of Oscar's doting love for me

together. Their friendship has actually always been
good; especially for Oscar and me. Meant we could fob
them off to one another and be left alone.

It's funny, there are times I do miss Robbie... in a
strange way.
Familiarity, I suppose.

It's clear to me that Robbie is still incredibly loyal to
Oscar, like a lovesick puppy.
Sad, pathetic creature.
He's fighting even now to get dear Oscar's finances
in order.

Now isn't THAT just precious.

Robbie is a very good gentleman – and EVERYONE
knows it and Oscar just loves him for it.

I just wish people would look at me for once and think
I am a good man and see all the joy I have brought to Oscar.

I was revered and adored by Oscar; I was taken
everywhere by him, introduced to everyone, unlike the
other boys. Oscar would grab me by the arm proudly
when entering a room and speak of me with such high

esteem. With his surprise gifts that I would receive and the endless love letters. He would bring me roses for no reason, other than saying that I was his morning!

Robbie found himself taken for granted, while I walked all over a ubiquitous red carpet laid out by my dear Oscar.

Robbie has never been in receipt of such grandeur... it now seems that he never will.

I still want Oscar to write about me in a story or play, publishing to the world how he feels about me! I want to be immortalised in his work.
I want to be at the centre of the world, and I got that from Oscar.

But it was always as Oscar's boy.
As a pretty bit of fluff sat beside him at dinner.

I was always in Oscar's shadow.
I fear now I always will be.

I thought that the time I put into being with him— however enjoyable—I would, I should get some success out of it for my writing at least.

Notability of some sort... but no, I am no beloved writer, not like him.

I can't be arsed to work, to write.
He was supposed to speed all that up for me, publishing deals and such...

And now I am stuck here in this godforsaken place with NOTHING.

In Exile.
ON MY OWN!

My life is nothing without Oscar!

*Beat.*

**BOSIE** *storms off stage.*

Is it too much to ask for a hot fucking tea?!

**END OF ACT ONE**

# Act Two

*BOSIE is in the bath, it is early evening. BOSIE exclaims to the hotel staff beyond his room.*

It is STILL not warm enough; it isn't too much to ask, is it? To indulge in a bath containing HOT water...?

It seems like the simplest of tasks is beyond them!

I hate it.

I hate all of it.

I hate everything.

I hate that if I have indecencies with someone today, I have to think, will there be repercussions tomorrow, or next week, or next month, or year?

I NEVER used to worry about that.

*BOSIE picks up a newspaper and reads.*

Even my title wouldn't protect me.

How I used to love the scrapes that Robbie and I would
find ourselves in...

Robbie's a social butterfly; friends all around town.

Robbie would recall to us all about his frequent relations.

Thomas, darling little thing, only fourteen.

Now this is where it got a little messy...
Robbie invited me to dine at his home one evening.
To my surprise, Thomas was standing proudly in the
drawing room awaiting my arrival.

He really was beautiful; light brown hair, clear
complexion, that nice standard petite frame.

It was a wonderful evening, the food, the conversation,
the sexual charge. I invited Thomas upstairs... with our
host's permission, of course, which he gave freely and
without hesitation. Good old Robbie, ever the sport.

I led Thomas up the stairs, I glanced back once or twice
to see his handsome face staring back up at me.
I started to feel my manhood grow in my bloomers
with excitement and anticipation.

But before we went into the bedroom, he asked me to introduce him to Oscar... the little tart. That's all they ever want. In the heat of the moment, I said, "I will".

I got him into that room and I made him— *(interrupts himself)* We had the most intimate and wonderfully passionate of times together.
Dominating another male makes me feel so powerful and alive!

But things got bad for Robbie and me when Thomas's parents became suspicious of "things" and of "goings on", they managed to get Thomas to confess to his sexual activity with Robbie and in the process, Thomas confessed his activities with me.

**BOSIE** *claps his hands.*

Well done, you dumb, young fool.

All of a sudden it was a whirlwind of panic, and meetings and the fear of being tossed to the police for bloody buggery, thrown in prison.

*(Reflectively)* I wonder if Oscar is lonely? I wouldn't be able to cope, sitting in mould. Mice and vagrants sitting beside me. This place is bad enough.

All it took was a little coercion. Thomas would be seen
as a perpetrator. Take it from me, he definitely was not
a victim in any way.

Thomas WAS equally guilty; with that he could face the
possibility of going to prison... when we raised this to
his parents' attention, I remember his mother Anita,
letting out a little whimper. We had won...

It's cruel, I know, but when you're a dog trapped in a
corner you have to bite, and hard.

Heard on the grapevine that Thomas was sent off to
boarding school not long after.

He must LOVE IT.

College is one long dream of joy.
A carnival of unbridled lust.

You know, it was at school where I flourished,
became a "sexual beast".
Sins of the flesh are not wrong!

My last term at Winchester, George Montagu. Four
years my junior, a fair-haired, blue-eyed, pretty boy with

engaging manners. Our mothers were great friends,
so I would stay at his family home.

George was so very… light…
I could throw him around like a rag doll. I was seventeen.
He really enjoyed it when I dominated, slap and tickle.
Daddy did give me some skills after all.
I dominate; I always do. Unless I need to get Oscar's
attention – then I have to be a little bitch.

I am determined to be manly.

*Beat.*

At school I cultivated insensitivity to pain, whenever
danger appeared, I'd rush out to meet it!
Fighting would break out in the courtyard at
lunchtimes, harmless scraps mostly, but I would be
there in a flash to throw my punches, not even knowing
what I was fighting for.
I did it so that everyone would see that I, Bosie,
was a man!

Such a rush of testosterone.

I put it down to the Greeks, they started it, and the
Romans, well… They perfected it.

Must have been so exciting, endless bloody fornicating.
The freedom. No judgement.


Isn't fair to have been born in such an oppressed time.

*He gets out of the bath.*

To go back to Ancient Greece!
Some of the undergraduates would have reproductions
of Simon Solomon on their walls... Hellenic
homosexuality, the thing of dreams!


When I left Winchester, I was eighteen, a man, and
I was truly ripe for any kind of wickedness!


Before I went to Oxford though, I was carted off to
France with a tutor, Gerald.
It was there that I had some of the best and most
intimate sex of my life.
I met a true beauty of a woman.
I am sure DADDY would be SO proud.
She was at least twelve years my senior, but ageless
and beautiful.
Slim and weak.
She was the divorced wife of an earl, an entrancing
countess.

My countess!

Look... I may fuck the servant boy, but I am not going to
fuck the maid.
A woman without a title isn't really a woman at all!

I had such control and power over her little body;
she had the same frame as my mother.

Such delicious fun, positively intriguing and a woman
no less.

It has to be said that a woman; well, women in general...
they're just child bearers, pretty things sat by their
husbands at dinner, they're just cooks, cleaners,
mothers, milk-filled breasts for their young.

BUT, be it noble or a sow, at the end of the day, a woman
is just a sloppy wet cunt for a man to fuck!
That thing slapped between a woman's legs, what
"most" men want, crave and desire... regardless of it
belonging to their own wife or not.

But, gripping a rock-hard cock is so fun.
Much more satisfying than plunging your fingers deep
into some moist quim.

I'm used to feeling a tight body, things being TIGHT,
not some sagging lady garden.

Desirable men are frequent, but those countesses
are a rare find.

All this fun with MY countess gave my tutor Gerald
terrible anxiety. He barged in on us one evening.
I was sent back to England quicker than you can say
"Timbuktu".

BOSIE *picks up male undergarments off the floor. They are
not his.*

I suppose he must have forgotten these; or perhaps he
left them. Like a calling card.
I picked up this chap this morning while buying flowers.
He caught my eye. I am like a magpie that way; I see
something pretty, I just have to HAVE it!

BOSIE *sniffs the pants deeply.*

Mmm, the sweet, potent, fresh smell of youth.
It's nice to see such a small pair. Oscar's are, well…

BOSIE *stretches the pants wide.*

…rather more for the portly gentlemen.

BOSIE *throws the pants on the floor.*

> And after Oscar has taken off his HUGE undergarments,
> his bottom, his bottom is so creased with lines and
> wrinkles you'd think his trousers were still on.

> In a couple of years, my looks will be just a distant memory.
> But to Oscar, I'll be perfect forever!

*Beat.*

> It was Robbie Ross who first introduced Oscar to renters
> and to Taylor, not me!
> I wouldn't be here and Oscar wouldn't be in prison if
> Robbie had never done that.

> Taylor was just tried and convicted alongside Oscar.
> He ran the brothel over by Westminster under the self-
> indulgent name of "Taylors", it was an amazing secret
> cavern of fun, boys of every variety, men of
> every station.
> A magnificent establishment! There should be one
> on every street corner!

A plainclothes police officer actually visited Taylors.

I was terrified, we all were. Taylor fled to some rooms in Chelsea. I suspect business took a fall in attendance.

It all seemed too risky for Oscar and me, and sadly no longer the fun kind of risky.
But Oscar plotted a way to avoid ANY danger and cut out the risk.
He took chambers of his own. St James's Place, ground floor, two-room chamber. Tastefully decorated, it would fill with such luminescent sunlight, a beautiful sanctuary.
He told his wife that he needed the place "purely to work undisturbed".
I was there every day. Of course.

Many young, handsome men would also visit Oscar's new chambers, some young male fans, some stableboys from Taylors.

One boy Oscar got from Taylors, a chap named Sidney; Oscar gave him a cigarette case inscribed with "Sidney from O.W".

*(Angrily)* He would give the boys of Taylors many gifts. I was furious with him about that!

I should be the one being showered with gifts.
Not these vagrants!
I suppose they are better looking. Or perhaps
MORE willing.
Oscar can be such a pig.
Why should I be shunned by the beast?
Really, I am the only one that's actually worthy
of any gifts from Oscar.

I saw that boy – Sidney. Or rather I saw the cigarette case.
He was pulling a cigarette out of it on the steps to the
court talking to my father's lawyer. I realised instantly
that he was going to give evidence AGAINST Oscar. I was
so close to attacking the little shit.
I cornered and threatened him; I grabbed him by the
scruff of the neck and promised that I would tell all the
queers of London that he is RIFE with syphilis.

Words can be so very powerful. Oscar taught me that!

Thankfully THAT threat to his livelihood convinced him
NOT to say anything and actually to tell the court that
his statement was false and that the police had scared
him into saying something.

He swore that Oscar had been nothing but a good friend
to him. It was a needed jolt to the prosecution.
I am now thankful for that ONE gift.

*Beat.*

I deserve more for being who I am, for all that I have done!

It's not like I am not a good person; I am.
I really am!

I am an incredibly generous person.

And if generosity doesn't show someone's good nature
and character, then what the hell does? I mean really.

Now for instance, this coat, to me, normally this would
only have a little more wear left in it.
Several more evenings perhaps.

So I would give it away, to a less fortunate soul.
Now if that's not charitable and good-spirited, then I
REALLY don't know what is.

Alas, I can no longer be quite so frivolous, what with
Oscar no longer here to get me the latest trends, and see
to my needs. Pay for my desires.

If he were here, I WOULD give this away. I'd love to.
If it meant I got a new one. Which it used to.

More than likely I would give this to one of the renters,
one of the many boys of Taylors, and the thanks I'd get
in return would leave me weak in my knees.

If I were to give this away today though, I'd be sure to
empty out all of the pockets.
I have learnt the hard way on leaving things in one's
pockets.
Not money or anything like that, but notes.

Love letters, from Oscar.

A love letter from Oscar Wilde is as valuable as a pocket
full of pound notes.

I gave one of the renters some clothing after "fun"
one evening.
He used a note that I had left in a jacket of mine to
blackmail us... well, him... Oscar.
He was going to go to the police with it. It wouldn't have
been a good situation if he had; this note contained such
whimsically lovely things about my soft, rose lips, and
the love he has for me. I doubt the police would have seen

it as anything other than perverted and scandalous.

I was careless... A terrible trait of mine, I admit.

Messy situations do so quickly appear, except, back
then they used to always seem so easy to clear up.
BUT NOT ANYMORE!

If you're not doing something that is worthy of being
blackmailed over, then you are simply NOT living.

Several weeks later, Oscar still had a love affair with that
same renter, even after all he did. Oscar paid him thirty-
five pounds in exchange for the letter... It's like there is
no shame.
And that renter had no problem explaining to the court
what took place between him and Oscar.

There are such despicable creatures in this world.

Thirty-five pounds isn't a great deal for Oscar to "throw
away"; he would spend more than that on me in a whim,
if he felt the urge to, or if I ever asked him to.
And for that some people call me spoiled.
I just like to have fun and I like to look good while having
that fun!

I'm perhaps still that spoiled child that Mother darling
raised me to be.

It's just that life can be such a bore...

PEOPLE can be such bores.

What terrifies me more than ANYTHING is to live a life
of normality. To become a husband, a father... I might as
well become a corpse and be buried now.
I see them, those people – living such an existence,
thinking that attending a dinner party with friends is
the highlight of one's social calendar. Fuck NO!
It scares me senseless.
Thank the lord for my title, for money, life, parties.
Life should be pleasure.

That is why I lived in London.
I know what I want.
I want EXCITEMENT!

I want to be somebody.

I am somebody with Oscar.

Life is happening with Oscar; I exist.

I'm alive.

People care about who I am.

THAT nourishes me, that feeling... not of being loved or adored by Oscar, but of being seen, of existing.

That feeling nourishes me more than food, more than sex!

*Beat.*

Oscar really is a most wonderful companion, but, sexually speaking, not to my taste.

Of course I can play the "little bitch" when required. Don't judge me. It's 1895; it's all tit-for-tat these days, and there's no going back.

I'm just wise enough to know it, and brave enough to bloody admit it!

Oscar has tits... sagging arse too.

Now, when I did not feel the obligation to keep Oscar happy and if we wanted 'physical' fun... we would just go out for it.

Bosie, by the way, my nickname, given to me by my mother. Mummy used it to call me her "little boy".

But be relieved, I am NO little "little boy" down there. *(Pointing to his crotch)* Where it counts. There I have had no complaints, or difficulties... Not like dear Oscar. He was happy to just watch on those limp evenings.

**BOSIE** *forces a fake 'sad face'.*

That's when I would be more than encouraged to play with boys.

The "renters" of London town are always young and just full of fire.
Oscar was accustomed to them and actually loved the time he had with them.
He described it perfectly once, saying, "it's like feeding with the pumas".
How right he was.

Oscar is a master with words. He could make one laugh and cry in an instant.

It's funny, when I converse with renters, or any of the poor, it's clear that they come from the gutter, but that really shouldn't be. They should mimic me, the way I talk, and the way I act. Their manners ought to be ten times better than mine, because they have had to study them... But no!

Not for this lot. Not at all.

When they talk, they all still sound like cats shrieking in an alley... That's why I make a point of giving them something to stick in their mouth quickly so I don't have to hear it.

When you pay, you don't need to care, you can be as rough as you like. Spit on them, laugh at them, cum and then kick them out...

It's strange, the one or two "loves" I've had, well, they make me want to do the opposite.
I want to hold them.
To be one with them.
It's different, it's delicate...

It satisfies a deeper part of me.
But then I still need that primal side of myself fulfilling it HAS to be satisfied—and I suppose—that's what the renters of this world are here for!

What is most amusing about the renters is the loyalty of them – or the lack of.
The same renters who were paid SO handsomely by Oscar, were the same renters who helped put him behind bars.

First Oscar paid them... for lustful fornication.

Then my father paid them... for providing—in detail—
the lauded details of those moments.

It's dirty.

Father reached his limit with the glamorous bubble that
contained Oscar and me, and wanted to burst it.
He didn't think that Oscar was someone with whom I
should be associated.
I am of age and free to choose my own friends.

Father called me a fool and a baby and called Oscar a
"hideous monster" and a "villain".

Mother even became worried about Father's maddening
insanity, so she had me packed off to Florence for a while.
Oscar was to join me later after completing some work.

But I got word from my brother, Percy, that our father
had barged in to Oscar's home with some henchman of
some variety and threatened that he would thrash Oscar
if he were to see me again.

Oscar is never good when confronted with violence.
Even on the occasion when I have shaken him, he has
curled into a ball.
Poor thing.

Oscar had his lawyer send a letter to my father asking
for an apology and for his behaviour to cease.
He replied with no apology.
Oscar was going to sue, but he knew how it would upset
my mother, so didn't.
He really is too compassionate.

When I returned from Florence, Father PUBLICLY
degraded Oscar and me; making the rounds of the
restaurants warning the waiters that he would thrash
Oscar if he saw him with me.

I armed myself with a revolver and told my father that if
I shoot him, it would be in self defence.
I accidentally fired the gun while on the roof of the
Berkeley Hotel... It caused such a commotion.

It's all play acting, if father really wanted to thrash
Oscar and me, he would have done it.

Father had me surrender the pistol to Oscar's lawyer,
and he insisted on never reading another letter from me
for as long as I live.
So... I took up the habit of sending him postcards
instead. Sometimes as many as ten a day!
He finally responded, calling me a reptile, saying that I
"was no son of his"... Now, if only that were true!

Father saw Oscar and me in Café Royale. He called us
"loathsome and disgusting".

Oscar became incredibly worried.
He felt that "a terrible danger was looming on the
horizon" ... "troubled days".

If only we knew just how troubled they were to become.

*Beat.*

It all came to a point when Father left a notecard for
Oscar at the desk of the Albemarle Club, it said "Oscar
Wilde, posing as a sodomite". The porter thankfully
placed the card in an envelope.

Oscar was so distressed.
He called Robbie to consult with and the three of us
were all adamant that something had to be done.

But I was the one who really pushed Oscar to go after my
father – to make him stop torturing me... us.

I pushed and I pushed, screaming hysterically about
what damage Father could do... Until Oscar caved in.
As he so often did.

Oscar agreed to sue my father. I am his own Darling Boy
after all. Oscar's lawyer reviewed the card, and after we
convinced him that it wasn't in the least bit true, charges
were brought about against Father for defamation.
Sadly, it was the first of many trials.

I have to admit, before all this business of the trials and
such... I was rather cooling on Oscar, but all the fight
and excitement—the determination to get my father—
well, it truly rekindled our spark!

Oscar was worried about the financial cost of
everything—as usual—so I convinced him that my
mother and family would be more than delighted
to pay... Sadly, I only managed to get together three
hundred and fifty pounds. He needed a lot more.
Thankfully, some friends of his, the Leversons, gave him
a loan of five hundred pounds.

Going into that courtroom with Oscar that first time, in hope
of successfully suing my father for libel, was so exciting!
We were so confident, we had proof, and it was Father
who was on shaky ground.
But... it all just backfired. My blinders were so strong
to what I wanted to happen. I was so angry and stupid.

I knew that the matter of the word "sodomite" would
come up and 'upset the apple cart' if you will.
But not in any dramatic way, certainly not in the way
that my father managed to prove it.

Taylor, and Oscar's association with him had been
found out and with that... all hope of winning.

Also, when Oscar was questioned, he lied blatantly
about his age, as he has ALWAYS DONE. Born in '54,
he replied that he was thirty-nine. He was forty-one.
A silly lie, but a lie nonetheless, and one too easy to prove.

Then there were renters that testified to Oscar's desire
for... unnatural relations.

My father had a well-informed detective garner the
most incriminating evidence against Oscar's
homosexual activity.

They had a list of boys that Oscar had committed "sodomy and other acts of gross indecency and immorality" upon. All the dates and locations going back more than a year...

My father had been planning and waiting for this! The catalogue of offences was too big a hurdle to beat. It was like watching a lamb to the slaughter.

One after another, the renters... the common tramps and whores paraded in front of that court of law and confessed to doing such things, having indecencies being performed upon them. Yet no charges brought about against them for their part in it all! It's madness.

Took the jury mere moments to decide on NOT GUILTY for the charges against my father.

The evening papers reported that Oscar Wilde was "damned and done for".

His friends and I all begged him to leave the country; we could have gone together, found a secluded spot, lived our life out together in peace.

He didn't listen.

Oscar was arrested. No bail. No hope.

He was detained in Holloway Prison.

I visited him EVERY DAY!

Fifteen-minute visits that were inhumane and barbaric
for all involved.

Oscar's a bit deaf you know, so what with the hellacious
shouting between the prisoners and the vagrants visiting
them, hearing one another was near to impossible.

So, we would sit. Staring at one another. Oscar with
tears streaming down his face.

He wrote daily, saying how seeing me each day made
his life bearable.

Oscar pleaded with me to leave the country.

To save myself.

But I stayed when ALL OTHERS left, like Robbie Ross.

I remained loyal, true, and ever loving.

I was still visiting Oscar daily... until I was practically
forced into exile!

It was Oscar's counsel—and Oscar—just before the
start of the second trial, they all pressed for me to leave.

Thinking that MY presence would make their task more
challenging!

The last time I saw Oscar... I had my hand on the iron
grate and Oscar kissed my finger. He said—we said—
that we would hold our love for one another.
The following day I left the country.
It was four days before the homosexual charges against
him commenced in court.

The first place I stayed, Calais, the Terminis Hotel, even
more disgusting than this.
I read reports on the trial in the daily papers coming
over from England, albeit twenty-four hours late. Oscar
also sent me daily letters.

I was—perhaps—a little insensitive in some of my
replies... saying how "Dieppe is the most depressing
place in the world", and how "Petits Chevaux was not to
be had as the casino's now closed" and it all being "such a
bore". I think I even wrote saying and how "France is like
the lowest hell of misery." Or something to that effect.
I can't imagine what he thought reading such things
while locked up in prison.

I've been much more tactful with my writing of late.
I've even started to write poetry again for the first time
in months!

*Beat.*

Thankfully Paris has better rooms on offer, on a budget.
I just felt so helpless here in France.
I wrote EVERY DAY to Oscar, begging him to let me
return and be a witness...

The jury disagreed on a verdict, so a new trial against
Oscar was set.
He was released on five thousand pounds bail.
That was when I made my way here.

I've gone from being in Oscar's "almost" constant
company for four years to suddenly NOTHING!
Here I can't seem to find a group, or social setting...
Friends.

I do like this hotel; I mean, they say I can stay as long
as I like without paying my bill, that is until I depart
– which is a good thing as I am quite penniless. The
proprietor is a very nice man indeed, most sympathetic
to my situation, and to Oscar's.

I miss my friends.

Father still doesn't believe that I've left London. He's
been blasting his way through the city looking for me.
The sad little man.

That third trial lasted for four days.

It was a repeat of everything Oscar had to endure from
the previous two. The same witnesses and stories.

I hear that Oscar was looking positively drained; the
papers reported that Taylor looked like a dug-up corpse.

It's strange, Oscar protects me by having me leave
England, and my father protects me by not implicating
me in the accusations.

To them both, I am just a victim of the other.

BOSIE *picks up the paper.*

The judge found Oscar guilty.
Said it was the worst case he has EVER had on trial
and that Oscar has corrupted young men in the most
hideous way.
Sentenced to two years' hard labour.

I needed to prove that my father had no bearing over

my life, no hold or power, and the cost of that... Oscar's freedom.

But I hear my father is positively drowning in legal costs.

A silver lining, I suppose.

Those boys that gave evidence, most of them I too had had "intimate" relations with!
I could have had just as steep a sentence.

All because of sex.

You really never know with whom you're keeping company.

Francis was right about us being beasts.
I think people are either beastly individuals—like Father—hating the world around them, or sexual beasts —like myself—loving all that is on offer. LIVING LIFE!

I believe my father to be jealous of all my sexual openness and fun that I engage in. You know, his new wife, Ethel Weeden—a sprig of a girl, barely eighteen years of age—well, she wants a divorce!
DUE TO "LACK OF CONSUMMATION"!

*Beat.*

> We do have madness in the family; there is a record of it all.
> I think a history of homosexuality too.
> My brother and I, but Uncle James—they say—was a
> queer fellow...

> Also, rumours about my grandfather, keeping his male
> servants closer than deemed "appropriate", having the
> most beautiful young men waiting on him hand and foot.
> And then there's my father's obsession with buggery.

> Grandfather having such beauty around him was just
> like me with the renters; hunting for the most beautiful!
> Too risky now.

> Because of it, I am disgraced.
> Because of it, Oscar is in prison.
> I'm EXILED!

> But... Oscar being in prison is rather exciting, I mean,
> what a magnificent story for him to be able tell others,
> to share!

But what about mine...

My story is worthy of being told, being shared.

I am extraordinary and I am special... on my own.

But my story is already so entwined with his, it's all
about him. It's never about me.


Oscar and I were once the toast of London town.

And how did it come to this?


Now I have nothing. What do I have? My writing?


My memories of the fun...

The warmth Oscar's smile gave me when I would see
him across a crowded room.

The comfort in knowing that he would always be there...
smiling back. To what end?


Now I'm a social outcast.


What is Oscar's love if I have nothing?

Am I nothing?


I miss Oscar.

BOSIE *shakes head "NO".*

I don't miss him. I miss who I am when I am at his side...

I am Oscar's Boy Bosie. Oh God.

*Beat.*

Right...

**BOSIE** *puts on his hat, begins to exit, then returns to pick up the paper.*

Are you still here?

**BOSIE** *exits.*

**END**

# bosie: informing an audience

This accompanying essay examines various aspects of Bosie (Lord Alfred Bruce Douglas) and his life. Research materials has included stage plays, screenplays, newspapers, essays, journals and autobiographies covering both primary and secondary sources.

Bosie is usually presented as narcissistic, self-obsessed, petulant and child-like, such as the depictions found in *Judas Kiss*,[1] *Wilde*[2] and *The Happy Prince*.[3] Bolstering character traits and assumptions. I aimed to develop a deeper understanding of his actions and behaviours, providing a fresh perspective on this character.

---

1    David Hare, *The Judas Kiss*, first edition (New York: Grove Press, 1998).
2    Brian Gilbert, *Wilde* (Sony Pictures Classics, 1997) <https://www.allmovie. com/movie/v158631> [accessed 7 June 2019].
3    Rupert Everett, *The Happy Prince (2018)* (Lionsgate, 2018) <https://www.imdb.com/title/tt2404639/> [accessed 7 June 2019].

# Locations

## Café Royal, Glasshouse Street, London

Bosie was accustomed to Café Royal, and would expect to be taken there for luncheon by Wilde.[4] Café Royal became a stage for Bosie and Oscar's love affair, blossoming within the private dining rooms. Wilde made sure that 'Bosie was taken to the Café Royal, Kettner's, the Savoy and lived, almost exclusively on, 'clear turtle soup', 'luscious ortolons wrapped in their crinkled Sicilian vine-leaves', 'amber-scented Champagne', 'pates procured directly from Strasberg', washed down with 'special cuvees of Perrier-Jouet',[5] bestowing decadence and delicacies upon him, Bosie 'was not only adored but revered'.[6] Bosie 'was already well versed in decadence'[7] and Wilde did nothing to dispel his expectation of grandeur, fine dinners, hotels, travel and boys. After Wilde's arrest in April, 1895, he called Bosie out on his 'incessant demands for money: your claim that all your pleasure should be paid for by me whether I was with you or not'.[8, 9]

4     Neil McKenna, *The Secret Life of Oscar Wilde* (New York: Basic Books, 2005), p. 275.
5     Rupert Croft-Cooke, *Bosie: Lord Alfred Douglas, His Friends and Enemies* (Indianapolis Ind.: Bobbs-Merrill, 1963), p. 59.
6     Croft-Cooke, p. 59.
7     Trevor Fisher, *Oscar and Bosie: A Fatal Passion*, first edition (Sutton Pub, 2002), p. 40.
8     Lewis Broad, *The Friendship and Follies of Oscar Wilde*, first edition (London: Hutchinson, 1954) p. 119.
9     Antony Edmonds, *Oscar Wilde's Scandalous Summer*, first edition (Stroud: Amberley, 2015), p. 18.

Not everyone enjoyed Café Royal, writer Thomas Burke —dismissive of the 'queer creatures' to be found there—said it was 'a grim and inauthentic place,' filled with 'young men with pink voices and pink socks fumbling with the arts'.[10] Wilde would entertain writers and renters there,[11, 12] leading 'a titillating double life' where his activities became 'more intimate, in small private dining rooms'.[13] Frank Harris recounts Wilde entertaining two 'quite common' youths, Wilde talking about the Olympic Games with them, detailing 'how the youths wrestled [...] nude, clothed only in sunshine and beauty'.[14] Harris couldn't stand to hear it and left.[15]

Bosie invited his father to have luncheon there with him and Wilde, the three conversed, drank, ate and Wilde beguiled the Marquess, if only briefly.[16, 17, 18] As time went on, the two were chastised publicly by Bosie's father[19] after witnessing the two dine there, defying his orders, 'his son had lapsed back into the old vile habits'.[20]

10    Jonathan Rose, *The Intellectual Life of the British Working Classes*, third edition, (New Haven: Yale University Press, 2021), p. 449.
11    Renter was a colloquialism for rent-boy or male prostitutes, (Murray, p. 43.).
12    Paul Baker, *Polari: The Lost Language of Gay Men*, Routledge Studies in Linguistics, first edition (Oxfordshire: Taylor & Francis, 2003).
13    Martin Fido, *Oscar Wilde*, first edition (Hamlyn, 1973), p. 79.
14    Juliet Gardiner, *Oscar Wilde: A Life in Letters, Writings and Wit* (Gill & Macmillan, 1995), p. 135.
15    McKenna, p. 232.
16    McKenna, p. 280.
17    Casper Wintermans, *Alfred Douglas: A Poet's Life and His Finest Work*, first edition (London: Peter Owen Publishers, 2007) p. 48.
18    Richard Ellmann, *Oscar Wilde*, first edition (London: Penguin, 1988) p. 393.
19    Wintermans, p, 162.
20    Ellmann, p. 393.

In spring of 1894, Café Royal was the arena for the fateful meeting between Wilde and the writer, Robert Hichens,[21, 22] the 30-year-old journalist who had ambitions to be a novelist. Hichens solidified all the details he needed for his scandalous book, The Green Carnation,[23] published anonymously on the 15th September 1894. A work of 'fiction', it was a clear portrait of Wilde and Bosie, 'parod[ying] the open secret of Wilde's relationship with [Bosie] through the leading characters',[24] much to the detriment of Wilde.[25]

## Alfred Taylor's Brothel, Little College Street, London

Living a decadent life, Bosie stayed at 'the Avondale Hotel in Piccadilly for ten days'[26] he indulged in 'lunch at the Holborn viaduct restaurant',[27] and all this was juxtaposed with Taylors, a safe haven for homosexuals, where young men could be 'picked up' for pleasure.

A den of iniquity run by Alfred Taylor, a gentleman who, having squandered an inheritance of over £45,000, rented

21   McKenna, p. 300.
22   Hichens, a writer Bosie met in Egypt, 1884, who Bosie had promised to introduce to Wilde upon his return, (Murray, p. 53).
23   Robert Hichens, Green Carnation, first edition (London: Icon Books, 1961).
24   Anne Varty and Oscar Wilde, A Preface to Oscar Wilde (London; New York: Longman, 1998), p. 30.
25   McKenna, p. 300.
26   Montgomery Hyde, Lord Alfred Douglas: A Biography (London: Methuen, 1984), p. 69.
27   Wintermans, p. 57.

rooms in Little College Street, London,[28] where older, wealthy gentlemen could meet youths and indulge in 'activities'.[29] Wilde and Bosie felt 'that they could devote themselves to endless play and extravagant hedonism'.[30] Taylors was a place to be free, where one could indulge in pleasures that were frowned upon by the rest of society. Bosie was excited and 'fascinated by young men who for a few pounds [...] would prostitute themselves'.[31] Homosexual men of all stations could indulge in hedonism, breaking down the preconceived Victorian notion of class and its divides. Pursuing transient relationships, competition would sometimes develop between Bosie and Wilde.[32] Wilde 'was conscious of the danger and delighted in it,'[33] '[Wilde's] social graces had widened the circle of his acquaintance. His friendship with [Bosie] extended it still further'.[34] The other patrons 'serve as a protective circle, allowing them to think that they are more fully accepted'.[35] However, Taylors was raided by police on a summer afternoon in August, numerous men were taken into custody, two of which were dressed as females, all were held under suspicion to commit 'homosexual activities.[95] Wilde wrote sympathetically

---

28    Wintermans, p. 56.
29    Wintermans, p. 56.
30    Fisher, p. 234.
31    Ellmann, p. 366.
32    Ellmann, p. 366.
33    Croft-Cooke, p. 57.
34    Broad, p. 121.
35    Erving Goffman, *Stigma: Notes on the Management of Spoiled Identity* (Middlesex: Penguin, 1968), p. 120.

to Taylor's partner,[36] displaying Wilde's sensibilities towards not just Taylor but also the establishment.

Before the trials, Taylor remained loyal to Wilde, refusing to give evidence against him.[37] Taylor stood alongside Wilde in the dock at the Old Bailey on 26th April, 1895, charged with twenty-five acts of gross indecency, including 'acting as a procurer for Wilde'.[38] Wilde and Taylor tried together was a 'nasty legal decision',[39] forcing Wilde to confirm visiting Taylor's, stating that it was for his amusement, a place to simply smoke a cigarette and listen to music,[40] and that he 'had met a number of young men there'.[41] The prosecution probed 'what possible gratification was it to you who, we are told, are a literary man to obtain the praise of these boys, whose very names you cannot remember?'[42]

It's crucial to clarify that Bosie scarcely knew Taylor, Wilde had developed a friendship with Taylor independent of Bosie. Despite this, Bosie still wanted to help with the 'unfortunate young man's defence', providing Taylors solicitor with £50 to support legal fees.[43]

---

36    Fido, p. 101.
37    Wintermans, p. 61.
38    Gardiner, p. 133.
39    Fido, p. 116.
40    Gardiner, p. 134.
41    'Trial of Oscar Wilde', *Aberdeen Journal* (Aberdeen, 27 May 1895) <http://tinyurl.galegroup.com/tinyurl/BYkyM4>.
42    'Trial of Oscar Wilde', *Aberdeen Journal* (Aberdeen, 27 May 1895) <http://tinyurl.galegroup.com/tinyurl/BYkyM4>.
43    Croft-Cooke, p. 125.

## Wilde's Home, 16 Tite Street, London

16 Tite Street was the home of Wilde, his wife Constance, and their two sons. They moved into this newly built home[44] and Wilde spent £5,000 of his wife's dowry having Edward William Godwin design the interior,[45, 46] creating the 'House Beautiful'.[47, 48] Important to note is that even Constance 'could not resist Bosie's appeal'.[49]

Their mutual friend, Lionel Johnson, introduced Bosie and Wilde to one another at Tite Street in 1891 and shortly after this successful meeting, the two had a second rendezvous. It's then that Wilde made sexual advances towards Bosie.[50]

Three years after that initial meeting on the 30th of June, 1894, the Marquess of Queensbury, Bosie's father, arrived without appointment at Tite Street, with a prize fighter.[51] The Marquess confronted Wilde, intimidating him, alluded to his homosexuality, 'I do not say that you are it, but you look it, and pose as it, which is just as bad. And if I catch you and my

---

44    English Heritage Charity, *Wilde, Oscar (1854–1900)* (2019) <https://www.englishheritage.org.uk/visit/blue-plaques/oscar-wilde/> [accessed 28 May 2019].

45    Fisher, p. 31.

46    Varty and Wilde, p. 65.

47    Anne Massey, *Biography, Identity and the Modern Interior (Radical Theologies)*, ed. by Penny Sparke, first edition (Abingdon-on-Thames: Routledge, 2013), p. 47.

48    Massey, p. 37.

49    Ellmann, p. 393.

50    Antony Edmonds, *Oscar Wilde's Scandalous Summer*, first edition (Stroud: Amberley, 2015), p. 15.

51    Merlin Holland, *The Wilde Album*, first edition (New York: Henry Holt and Company, 1998), p. 151.

son again in any public restaurant, I will thrash you.'[52] Wilde
wrote to Bosie saying how intolerable it was to be dogged by
a maniac.[53]

As soon as the press reported on Wilde's homosexuality,
his wife, Constance, took their sons out of school and left the
country. Wilde would never 'see his nine-year-old and eight-
year-old boys' ever again.[54] A friend of his and benefactor,
Helen Carew, went on to educate the boys on Wilde's
work, 'from which they had been kept apart, after Oscar's
imprisonment'.[55]

After the trial, on 24th April 1895, Tite Street hosted an
auction of Wilde's possessions.[56] Bosie wrote how 'the house
in Tite Street was no longer [Wilde's], and his furniture and
goods had all been seized and sold under distraint to satisfy
his creditors, within a week or two of his arrest'.[57] Wilde
was anguished, 'all my charming things are to be sold [...]
at give-away prices.'[58] Everything, from his writing desk to
the children's rabbit hutch was sold off.[59] The auction was

52    Students' Academy, *Victorian Novelists Series-Fifteen-Oscar Wilde*, first
      edition (USA: Independently published, 2011), p. 47.
53    Wintermans, p. 47–48.
54    Joseph Bristow, 'The Blackmailer and the Sodomite: Oscar Wilde on Trial',
      *Feminist Theory*, 17.1 (2016), pp. 41–62, p. 45.
55    James Robinson, 'Oscar Wilde's Friend and Benefactor, Helen Carew (c.
      1856–1928)', *Dublin Historical Record*, 58.2 (2005), 112–21, p. 112.
56    Varty and Wilde, p. 31.
57    Leslie Stokes and Sewell Stokes, *Oscar Wilde: A Play*, first edition (New
      York: Random House, 1938), p. 11.
58    Gardiner, p. 133.
59    Varty and Wilde, p. 231.

insufficient in covering the debts accrued from his legal battle causing great financial difficulty for the family.[60] Bosie initially promised to help pay Wilde's court fees but then let him down, resulting in the auction. Some of Wilde's property had been looted,[61] including the manuscript of *A Florentine Tragedy*, several of Wilde's friends managed to acquire several of his books and manuscripts, smuggling them out before the bailiffs arrived.[62] Bosie was not part of this effort.

## The Hotel des Deux Mondes, 22 Avenue de l'Opera, Paris

Bosie left for Calais the day before Wilde's trial as his presence was 'prejudicial to the chances of acquittal'.[63] In late May, 1895, Bosie arrived at The Hôtel des Deux Mondes.[64] He'd previously stayed there with Wilde.[65] In December, 1894, Bosie had ventured to Egypt, but felt neglected by Wilde, so, by March Bosie begged Wilde to meet in Paris. Wilde refused, so Bosie wrote a telegram, hinting at suicide, stating that he would rather die than spend a life without him. Wilde hurried to him. In Paris, the two reconciled, their bond and

---

60    Fisher, p. 127.
61    Norbert Kohl, *Oscar Wilde: The Works of a Conformist Rebel*, first edition
      (Cambridge: Cambridge University Press, 2011), p. 275.
62    Nicholas Frankel, *Oscar Wilde: The Unrepentant Years*, first edition,
      (Cambridge: Harvard University Press, 2017), p. 233.
63    Bernard Shaw, Alfred Bruce Douglas, and Mary Hyde Eccles, *Bernard
      Shaw and Alfred Douglas, a Correspondence*, first edition (London: John
      Murray, 1982), p. xvi.
64    Ellmann, p. 372.
65    Hyde, p. 87.

love was reaffirmed, having dinner at Voisin's and supper at Paillard's.[66] Wilde spent lavishly, £85 in just restaurants,[67] he enabled a 'disastrously extravagant lifestyle with Bosie',[68] giving into Bosie's demands and expectations.

In September 1894, Wilde had written to Bosie saying how he was longing for France, and to be with him,[69] but within a year of this request Bosie found himself alone and in exile. During the trial the judge stated that Bosie 'went to Paris at the request of the defendant, and there he has stayed, and I know absolutely nothing more about him'.[70] The hotel permitted Bosie to stay without paying his bill till his departure, which was a good thing as he felt quite penniless, Bosie felt that the proprietor was a very nice man and most sympathetic to his situation and Oscar's.[71]

66      Wintermans, p. 39.
67      Gardiner, p. 115.
68      Holland, p. 145.
69      Oscar Wilde, Merlin Holland, and Rupert Hart-Davis, *The Complete Letters of Oscar Wilde*, first edition (New York: Henry Holt, 200), p. 369.
70      Fisher, p. 144.
71      Wilde, Holland, and Hart-Davis, p. 396.

# Family

Bosie's family, English aristocracy with unconventional behaviour, a 'Victorian melodrama',[20] the Marquess would boast about his sexual exploits to his wife and even suggested she join him and his mistress, and the three of them live together. The Marquess 'expressed a distaste for his entire family'[72] resulting in Bosie's mother, Sibyl, diverting her love and attention from her husband and onto Bosie. Then, Bosie's brother, Francis, another homosexual, who was pushed to suicide by their father, which left Bosie grief-stricken and angry.

Castrated by the Marquess through financial control, Bosie struggled with relationships where the balance of power wasn't in his favour. Sigmund Freud detailed that 'a son (in absence of a loving and nurturing relationship with their father) will actively engage in the direct desire to remove their father'.[73] Bosie was treated with contempt by his father, the Marquess had a sadistic nature to the abuse he inflicted, his 'favourite means of taunting his sons was to suggest that he had not fathered them'.[74] Writing retrospectively on Bosie

---

72    David Schulz, 'Redressing Oscar: Performance and the Trials of Oscar Wilde', TDR (1988–), 40.2 (1996), 37–59, p. 47.
73    Freud, Sigmund, *Group psychology and the analysis of the ego*. In J. Strachey (Ed. and Trans.), *The standard edition of the complete works of Sigmund Freud* (Vol. 18) (London: Hogarth Press, 1955) pp. 67–143.
74    Douglas Murray, *Bosie: A Biography of Lord Alfred Douglas*, first edition (New York: Hyperion, 2000) p. 56.

wearing an iron brace, the Marquess said that it made him 'sick to look at [Bosie] and think that he could be called my son'.[75, 76] His fragile ego despised what had spawned from his own loins.[77]

## Power plays in Bosie's father-son relationship

Bosie and his father 'were well matched [...] each knew how best to wound the other; their insults were as calculated as they were vindictive'.[78] Their correspondence became 'childish and undignified', leading to Bosie threatening murder; there was a theatrical nature to the family but homicidal intentions were a new low.[79] Bosie said that if the Marquess—referred to as being 'a violent and dangerous rough'—assaulted him or Wilde, he'd have no option but to defend himself using the loaded revolver which he always carried, and that if he shot him it'd be in self-defence and completely justified. He added that very few people would actually miss the Marquess if he were to die.[80] The Marquess demanded Bosie relinquish the weapon to his solicitor else he'd inform the police. Before succumbing, Bosie fired it off the roof of the Berkeley Hotel. During another one of their

---

75   Worn by Bosie to rectify his knocked knees, (Croft-Cooke, p. 26.).
76   Croft-Cooke, p. 26.
77   Croft-Cooke, p. 26.
78   Brian Roberts, *The Mad Bad Line : The Family of Lord Alfred Douglas*, first edition (London: H. Hamilton, 1981), p. 188.
79   Edmonds, p. 67.
80   Hyde, p. 61.

arguments, the Marquess said he'd never read another letter
from him. In retaliation, Bosie sent postcards instead.

At the age of fourteen, the Marquess' own father died,
making him the 'owner of a large estate and the nominal
head of his family', the new Marquess of Queensberry.[81]
The Marquess never possessed self-restraint and 'could
now assert himself with authority'.[82] He garnered not only
status, but also power, this 'instant elevation to the Scottish
peerage did nothing to balance his already lop-sided
personality'.[83] Some men feel the need to 'constantly assert
their power and virility by showing off'.[84] The Marquess did
this by parading his sexual exploits and bullying his family.
Bosie's father was headstrong, even changing the rules of
boxing, implementing The Queensberry's Rules, still used
today.[85] The Marquess suffered from a 'fragile ego and bad
temper',[86] fiery, head-strong and lacking in self-control.[87]
The Marquess was a man who 'was driven to persecute
others',[88] his wife and their children endured continuous
abuse.

---

81    Roberts, p. 25.
82    Roberts, p. 25.
83    Roberts, p. 25.
84    Rosalind Minsky, *Psychoanalysis and Gender: An Introductory Reader*, first
      edition (London: Routledge, 2002), p. 37.
85    Scott Beekman, *Ringside: A History of Professional Wrestling in America*, first
      edition (Westport: Praeger, 2006), p. 32.
86    Roberts, p. 25.
87    Croft-Cooke, p. 25.
88    Roberts, p. 149.

The Marquess 'could, when it suited him, be charming but, when crossed, he became truculent and abusive'.[89] He 'would use any means to humiliate',[90] and unfortunately for Bosie as Ellen DeLara states, 'the consequences of bullying last into adult lives'.[91] The Marquess had unparalleled 'belligerence and [...] litigiousness. He had made himself known as a fulminate against Christianity, and was always raging publicly and indecorously against someone else's creed. He fancied himself as an aristocratic rebel, socially ostracised because of his iconoclasm.'[92] The Marquess denounced Christianity resulting in him getting ejected from the House of Commons.[93]

The Marquess held financial power over Bosie. Denying his allowance was a regular power play, but Bosie was happy to forfeit his yearly £250 allowance from his father in exchange for his continued relationship with Wilde, feeling that 'any sacrifice was worthwhile if it annoyed his father'.[94] Bosie was financially supported by his mother and grandfather, Wilde too claimed that he had spent over £5,000 entertaining Bosie.

Animosity built between the Marquess and Wilde, the

---

89      Roberts, p. 25.
90      Roberts, p. 149.
91      Ellen DeLara, *Bullying Scars : The Impact on Adult Life and Relationships*, first edition (Oxford: Oxford University Press, 2016), p.xi.
92      Ellmann, p. 365.
93      Croft-Cooke, p. 31.
94      Roberts, p. 188.

Marquess calling Wilde a 'sodomite'[95] and Bosie encouraging Wilde to pursue a libel suit.

## Overindulged nature in Bosie's mother-son relationship

Born in 1870, Bosie became the most important person to his mother, Sibyl, starved of affection from her absent husband. She lived in rented accommodation amongst strangers, clinging to Bosie with a ferocious possessiveness.[96] Sibyl 'called him by the West-Coast diminutive 'Boysie', meaning 'little boy'.[97]

Sibyl, rejected by her husband neurotically clung to Bosie.[98] The Marquess was explosive in his youth and once married, his wife experienced this first-hand, as did their children.[99] Kathryn Hughes states that 'women were considered physically weaker yet morally superior to men'.[100] The Marquess 'liked to brag about his conquests, to flaunt his mistresses',[101] not only to his friends but also to Sibyl... being a woman of standing, she found this difficult to address and deal with, resulting in

---

95      Merlin Holland, *The Real Trial of Oscar Wilde : With an Introduction and Commentary*, first edition (New York: Perennial, 2004), p. xix.
96      Roberts, p. 67.
97      Murray, p. 12.
98      Seward, p. 169.
99      Roberts, p. 149.
100     Kathryn Hughes, 'Gender Roles in the 19th Century' <https://www.bl.uk/romantics-andvictorians/articles/gender-roles-in-the-19th-century> [accessed 7 June 2019].
101     Roberts, p. 72.

their relationship having 'unbearable complications'.[102] Without any option she filed for divorce on the grounds of adultery and cruelty.[103, 104] Important to note that legislation brought in at this time, the Matrimonial Causes Act of 1857, enabling a man to divorce his wife on the grounds of adultery alone, whereas wives could only divorce their husbands if there had been 'exacerbated adultery with other offences.'[105] In Sibyl's case the "other offences" were the bullying she endured. But the bullying continued even after the divorce, Sibyl 'could not escape him. The more he was shunned by society, the more obsessive became his hatred for his wife and her family. 'My father', declared Bosie, 'was a madman, and his mania was to persecute my mother'.[106]

Bosie witnessed his parents' turbulent relationship, and how 'heterosexual ideals are impossible to attain in any absolute sense'.[107] He feared those parental arguments that would leave his mother in tears.[108] Bosie developed a protectiveness over his mother, siding with her in any row, she would then do the same for him. Sybil went as far as begging the University of Oxford to award Bosie his degree,

---

102    Margaret Mead, *Male and Female. A Study of the Sexes in a Changing World*. (Penguin: Harmondsworth, 1962), p. 339.
103    Murray, p. 18.
104    Croft-Cooke, p. 37.
105    Holly Furneaux, 'Victorian Sexualities' <https://www.bl.uk/romantics-andvictorians/articles/victorian-sexualities> [accessed 7 June 2019].
106    Roberts, p. 148.
107    Nikki Sullivan and J. R. Cadwallader, *A Critical Introduction to Queer Theory*, first edition (Edingburgh: Edingburgh University Press, 2014), p. 91.
108    Roberts, p. 149.

even though he left without sitting his final exams, just like his father.[109]

For Sibyl, '[Bosie] became the centre of her world, her refuge from her husband's neglect, the solace for her frustrated emotions',[110] Bosie was aware of this, he wanted to be adored and needed by everyone, 'Freud distinguished between two types of love: narcissistic love, characterised by the desire to be loved, and analytical love, characterised by the desire to love'.[111] Bosie was a narcissistic lover, desiring to be loved, whereas Wilde was more of an analytical lover.

Minsky states how 'the danger with relationships based on narcissism is a part of our unconscious identity is projected onto someone else in the external world which makes us very vulnerable if that person rejects us',[112] Bosie attached himself to Wilde, affiliating himself with Wilde's achievements, developing a grandiose idea of himself. 'Bosie had been hopelessly spoilt by his mother and used to his own way',[113] making personal relationships challenging unless they were on Bosie's terms. Aware of this, Wilde entertained these notions, pandering to Bosie's every need, much as Sibyl did.

Sibyl loved Bosie more than her other children, but she felt that 'Bosie showed his father's cussedness. This

---

109    Hyde, p. 6.
110    Roberts, p. 67.
111    Minsky, p. 38.
112    Minsky, p. 39.
113    Roberts, p. 50.

'pig-headedness, this tendency to parade weaknesses as strengths, was all part of an ominous family trait'.[114] Bosie could be very aggressive, have a reckless nature[115] and could 'fly into a temper at the slightest provocation'.[116] Both Sybil and Wilde would pander to Bosie's outbursts, reenforcing his reckless behaviour.

## Homosexuality in Bosie's family

Tom Whipple states that 'homosexuality can be considered a universal phenomenon' with regards to it occurring throughout nature[117]; Victorian consciousness didn't have this viewpoint. The Wilde trials played a crucial role in 'fashioning the image of an unforeseen, distinctly modern type of homosexual identity'.[118] Francis, Bosie's older brother, had his homosexual relationship end abruptly due to the Marquess' meddling and abuse, Lord Rosebery, Francis's partner, was loathed by the Marquess as much as Wilde. Francis' death was classed as an accident rather than suicide.[119] The post-mortem report stated that 'the charge had entered the mouth, fracturing the lower jaw on the right side, and passing through the roof of the mouth on the left-

---

114    Roberts, p. 188.
115    Michael Patrick Gillespie, 'Bosie Biography', *English Literature in Transition*, 1880–1920, Volume 44, Number 4, 2001, 503–504, p. 504.
116    Croft-Cooke, p. 346.
117    Tom Whipple, *X and Why: The Rules of Attraction: Why Gender Still Matters*, first edition (London: Short Books, 2018), p. 128.
118    Bristow, p. 52.
119    Murray, p. 68.

hand side. Death must have been instantaneous'.[120] After being so close to his brother, Bosie was struck hard and left deeply saddened by Francis' sudden and unexpected death.[121] This, however, didn't stop him utilising the tragic event to coerce Wilde into meeting, threatening to kill himself if Wilde refused.

Additionally, there were rumours about Bosie's maternal grandfather's involvement in homosexual activities.[122] Further displaying just how frequently-occurring homosexuality is, even within Bosie's own family.

## Impotence and anger in Bosie

Georgene Seward explores how impotence can 'decrease the individual's general feeling of adequacy'.[123] Bosie's father, the Marquess, suffered with impotence.[124] In October 1884, the Marquess married Miss Ethel Weedon, a seventeen-year-old, who, after a fortnight, left him, due to his inability to consummate the marriage.[125] In 1994, when the divorce records were made public,[126] showed that none of Weedon's family were present at the ceremony and that the Marquess lied about her age, stating that she was over twenty-one...

---

120    Roberts, p. 183.
121    Croft-Cooke, p. 108.
122    Hyde, p. 8.
123    Georgene Seward, *Sex and the Social Order*, second edition (Middlesex: Pelican, 1954), p. 196.
124    Roberts, p. 181.
125    Croft-Cooke, p. 96.
126    Roberts, p. 182.

Bosie knew her real age and relished the opportunity to call his father a child-snatcher.[127]

'[Bosie] was a many-sided, complex young man. Gregarious, lively, given to wild enthusiasms and boisterous friendships, he seemed on the face of things to be the very antithesis of his surly father [...] Left to himself, he could become as sullen, moody and self-obsessed as any member of his family. His sudden outbursts of anger were as frightening as they were unpredictable. Indeed, his mother always maintained that, of all her sons, Bosie was the only one "afflicted with the fatal Douglas temperament".'[128] It is true that 'Bosie liked to boast that he had "the Douglas fighting blood and spirit"'.[129] Nothing exemplifies that spirit more than the fight he thrust in Wilde's hands against the Marquess. The Marquess went as far as to pay the witnesses for their accounts, aiding the prosecution against Wilde and securing a guilty verdict. 'Witnesses each received [£5] a week during the period [of] Wilde's arrest and his convictions'.[130] The Marquess was compelled not to lose this fight. Wilde was merely a pawn between father and son, being played by them both.

---

127    Roberts, p. 182.
128    Roberts, p. 153.
129    Roberts, p. 158.
130    Edmonds, p. 89–90.

# Sexuality

The Labouchere Amendment, introduced in 1895, was intended to protect women and female prostitutes. However, law also stated that 'any' act between two men, could be prosecuted as a criminal offence, even if there was no confirmation of anal intercourse. Prior to this amendment of the law, anal copulation was the only criminal sex act between two men. This amendment was an attempt to regulate male behaviour, exhibiting the Victorian prudery of the time.[131] Being found guilty of indulging in homosexual activities was socially damning, financially crippling and life changing. The law at this time made the lives of homosexual men difficult.[132] Historical sexual freedom, the Romans' open 'acceptance of sex of all sorts',[133] commented on by the character who longed 'to go back to ancient Greece'.[134] Revelling in homosexual activities at school, where 'homosexual activity was rampant'.[135] Victorian prudishness, ignorance and misunderstanding of the line 'love that dare not speak its name' from the poem 'Two Loves',[136] a poem, penned by Bosie, referred to as odious

---

131    Schulz, p. 47.
132    Robert William Burnie, *The Criminal Law Amendment Act, 1885. With Introduction, Commentary and Forms of Indictments*. (London: Waterlow & Sons, 1885).
133    Valentine Hooven and Angelika Muthesius, *Beefcake: The Muscle Magazines of America 1950–1970*, first edition (Koln: Taschen, 1995), p. 9.
134    Rik Barnett, *Bosie*. (London: Polari Press, 2024), p. 46.
135    Murray, p. 14.
136    Murray, p. 55.

for alluding to homosexual relations during the trial against Wilde.[137] Interestingly, that the word "homosexual" is first recorded being used in 1869 by Karoly Bankert during a heated exchange about sodomy laws in Germany.[138]

Despite the Victorian sexual repression, the press and readers remained voyeuristically fascinated about the courtroom drama surrounding Wilde's homosexual activity. Wilde admitted that he 'experienced violent, contradictory and disturbing feelings about his sexual and emotional attraction to young men, swinging between feelings of ecstasy and degradation, sexual exultation and remorse'.[139] While Wilde had felt conflicted about his homosexual behaviours,[140] Bosie did not.

Robert Ross and Wilde met in 1886 and became incredibly close.[141] Rupert Croft-Cooke notes that 'Ross was the most single-minded in [his] exhibitionistic devotion, and, until Wilde met Bosie, the most successful' in garnering Wilde's attention.[142] The closeness between the two bolstered Bosie's jealousy towards Ross. The character calls Ross a 'quim',[143] a Victorian colloquialism to describe female genitalia.[144]

---

137   Fisher, p. 114.
138   Michael King and Annie Bartlett, 'British Psychiatry and Homosexuality', *The British Journal of Psychiatry : The Journal of Mental Science*, 175 (1999), 106–13, p. 106.
139   McKenna, p. 48.
140   McKenna, p. 48.
141   Gardiner, p. 157.
142   Croft-Cooke, p. 50.
143   Barnett, p. 36.
144   Eric Partridge and Paul Beale, *A Concise Dictionary of Slang and Unconventional English*, first edition (London: Routledge, 1999), p. 950.

## Negative perceptions on Bosie

Including the details of Bosie sleeping with a fourteen-year-old boy could potentially bolster negative ideas and perceptions of gay men, but this sexual encounter displays 'the predatory indiscretions of [Bosie]'.[145] Having sex with someone this age isn't out of the ordinary for the 1890s. It was considered normal among his contemporaries; Thomas would've been equally guilty in a court of law, regardless of his age. While crafting his work, Kaufman 'worried about imposing his individual, postmodern-era views onto historical material, and suppressing diversity of perspectives on the [original] events',[146] I felt it important to include this event.

Bosie enjoyed being a 'homosexual', a term first coined in the 1880s.[147] He sought out homosexual pleasures; however, in later life he turned to Christianity and declared himself a heterosexual, blaming the homosexual nature of his youth, the fault of others who had led him astray and against his will. In 1918 Bosie blamed Wilde, referring to him as having 'a diabolical influence on everyone' and that he was 'the greatest force for evil in Europe for the last three hundred and fifty years'.[148]

---

145    Patrick Mason, 'Acting Out', *Irish University Review*, 32.1 (2002), 137–47, p. 140.
146    Shelley Salamensky, 'Re-Presenting Oscar Wilde: Wilde's Trials, Gross Indecency, and Documentary Spectacle', *Theatre Journal*, vol. 54 no. 4, (2002), 575–588, p. 576.
147    Furneaux.
148    Shaw, Douglas, and Hyde, p. xxxv.

Bosie craved control, wanting influence over others around him. Rosalind Minsky explores how castration anxiety can cause obsessional neurosis, this obsessional neurosis can make a man crave order and control.[149] When there was a lack of control, Bosie would become unhinged. Trevor Fisher explored how after some time apart, the balance of power between the two had shifted 'In the battle of wills, [Bosie] now had the upper hand. [Wilde] had gone reluctantly to meet him in Paris, it resumed a relationship on Bosie's terms.'[150] Wilde's friends felt that Bosie monopolised him and in later years, Wilde stated that Bosie had a 'greed for money: [caused] incessant and violent scenes: [and had] unimaginative selfishness'.[151]

## Bosie's homosexuality

At school Bosie overcame an 'initial reluctance "to do what everyone else did," he found himself doing it and giving in to the pleasures of homosexual relations, stating that 'at least ninety percent of the boys at Winchester were giving themselves over to the same thing'. Most of the boys would cease their homosexual pleasures once leaving school; Bosie didn't.[152] It is noted that 'homosexuality is not a question of complementary assertiveness, but a search for as much

---

149    Minsky, p. 60.
150    Fisher, p. 79.
151    Fisher, p. 235.
152    Roberts, p. 150–151.

maleness as possible',[153] Bosie sought to dominate, to be manly and less effeminate, he worried extensively that people may perceive him as effeminate.

Wilde was 'unusually tall, broad, and robust',[154] Bosie wasn't interested in him sexually, using sex as a tool to gain Wilde's attention. 'Their association was not as romantic as it was made to appear. Sexually incompatible, each sought other diversions. And the diversions they pursued were often hazardous',[155] diversion such as renters from Taylor's. Wilde was 'revolted and repulsed' by sex with his wife, Constance,[156] telling her that he had previously contracted syphilis and a recurrence of this had meant sex was impossible.[157] Holly Furneax confirms that 'sex was spoken everywhere in the 19th century in a wide range of contexts including the law, medicine, religion [and education]'.[158]

During this time it was normalised behaviour for many respectable young men to seek pleasure from prostitutes.[159] Margaret Mead writes, 'Male sexuality seems originally focused to no goal beyond immediate discharge',[160] and Bosie believed that 'sins of the flesh were not sins at all [...] sex was

---

153    Mead, p. 85.
154    Salamensky, p. 577.
155    Roberts, p. 190.
156    McKenna, p. 162.
157    Fisher, p. 33.
158    Furneaux.
159    Hughes.
160    Margaret, p. 215.

virtuous and life-affirming',[161] reflecting his fearless nature in a time of righteousness. Bosie mirrored his father's view on religion, the Marquess was a staunch atheist and described organised religion as 'Christian tomfoolery'.[162]

In the past, it was felt that 'penile-anal intercourse is physically disordered and it causes physical harm as well [...] the desire to engage in such actions is disordered. Since desires occur at the "mental" or "thought" level, it follows that such male homosexual desires are mentally discorded'.[163]

Bosie and Wilde were subjected to the 'notion of the homosexual as doomed to a life of torment, suffering and loneliness',[164] Bosie endured this rhetoric from society and his father. Wilde's trials dismantled and '[cleared] the way for a more "open atmosphere"'.[165]

Bosie went on to comment on how the homosexual acts Wilde engaged in were 'perversions to which Wilde was addicted'.[166] It's important to note that when Bosie wrote about Wilde, he did so from a place of defending himself.[167] In later life, Bosie denied his homosexuality and in March 1904, he married a young woman and fellow poet, Olive Custance.[168]

---

161   Neil McKenna *The Secret Life of Oscar Wilde* (New York: Basic Books, 2005), p. 156.
162   Hyde, p. 13.
163   L. Kinney, p. 385.
164   Sullivan and Cadwallader, p. 18.
165   Varty and Wilde, p. 30.
166   Douglas, p. 182.
167   Douglas, p. 298.
168   Roberts, p. 288.

The marriage consisted of difficulties, Custance was unfaithful and his new father-in-law didn't like him.[169] In 1902 they had a son, Raymond.[170] A decade after their marriage Bosie turned to Christianity, taking a vow of chastity, aiming for sainthood but settling for celibacy. This propelled his prejudice against homosexuality.[171] Bosie turned violently against Wilde,[172] surmising in his autobiography, 'all my life, from twenty years of age up, has been overshadowed and filled with scandal and grief through my associations with this man, Oscar Wilde'.[173] Towards the end of his life Bosie turned to Christianity and once reflected on Wilde, that he was 'cruelly and unjustly treated and whose brilliant genius, if he had not been condemned by an ungrateful country to prison and resulting in an early death, would have enriched the English stage with many more masterpieces of dramatic art',[174] and that 'if his fellow countrymen had treated [Wilde] with more Christian Spirit, he would have written half a dozen more comedies',[175] Yet another example of Bosie's pendulum-like feelings regarding Wilde.

---

169     Wintermans, p. 137.
170     Hyde, p. 144.
171     Roberts, p. 289.
172     Porter, p. 52.
173     Douglas, p. 296.
174     Stokes and Stokes, p. 11.
175     Stokes and Stokes, p. 12.

## Bosie and Ross

Wilde was a man who didn't just have friends but disciples, disciples like Robbie Ross.[176] Ross was a Canadian who had lived in England from the age of two. He was a gentleman who was very experienced in homosexual practices[177] and became one of Wilde's closest friends.

Wilde wrote to Ross, confiding in him about the Marquess, the calling card, how 'his whole life seems ruined by this man. The tower of ivory assailed by a foul thing. On the sand is my life split. I don't know what to do.' Ross discouraged legal action.[178] Wilde, in 1897, acknowledged Ross's loyal friendship, writing that 'I couldn't spoil your life by accepting the sweet companionship you offer me from time to time. It is not for nothing that I named you in prison St Robert of Phillimore [the London square where Ross lived]. Love can canonise people. The saints are those who have been most loved...' Ross left for France sooner than Bosie and still fought tirelessly to get Wilde's finances in order while abroad. Bosie took no action to help in these matters.[179]

The loyalty Ross had for Wilde is evident, even in the lead up to Wilde's release, Ross helped to raise £800 for him.[180] Even when Wilde passed away, Ross remained by Wilde's

---

176     Hyde, p. 41.
177     Fido, p. 79.
178     Gardiner, p. 122.
179     Gardiner, p. 155.
180     Gardiner, p. 150.

side until the very end, Bosie was absent and after Wilde's death,[181] Ross became Wilde's literary executor.[182] In later years, the hostility felt towards Ross remained the same and Bosie would publicly and persistently denounce Ross 'as a sodomite and a bugger'.[183] Bosie always felt that Wilde's mind and heart had been turned against him.[184]

## The desire for excitement

Bosie and Wilde were promiscuous and indulged in male renters, 'Wilde and [Bosie] were in the habit of swapping their young men'.[185] Wilde wrote, referring to Bosie, lying on the sofa like a hyacinth and worshipping him.[186] The hyacinth flower stands erect, referring to Bosie's erect penis, Wilde then worshipping it, performing oral sex upon him. Wilde had said to one male lover that 'love is a sacrament that should be taken kneeling',[187] Freud thought narcissism transfers to 'the sexual object';[188] Minsky further explored this 'object' as representing 'identity from pleasurable sensations from somebody – mouth, anus or genitals'.[189] Love is a sexual transaction, an ideology passed from Wilde to Bosie, Bosie's

---

181     Gardiner, p. 155.
182     Merlin Holland, *The Wilde Album*, first edition (New York: Henry Holt and Company, 1998), p. 126.
183     McKenna, p. 187.
184     Fido, p. 130.
185     Murray, p. 35.
186     Hyde, p. 29.
187     McKenna, p. 186.
188     Sigmund Freud. Ed. James Strachey Freud, 'Sigmund Freud, "On Narcissism: An Introduction"' (London: Hogarth Press, 1955), pp. 87–91, p. 88.
189     Minsky, p. 38.

thirst for sexual encounters that fulfil him, how being seen
and existing is important to him. Bosie described his own
sense of humour as superb.[190] Victorians maintained a rigid
and repressed façade, 'a veneer of respectable society over an
underbelly of prostitution and pornography'.[191]

## Submissiveness in Bosie

'It was far more acceptable to sodomise another man, or even
better, a beardless, androgynous boy, than to allow oneself to
be sodomised'.[192] Bosie being happily passive during a sexual
encounter is rare; but in a letter sent from Bosie to Maurice
Schwabe, who Bosie loved fondly, detailed that 'I really love
you far more than any other boy in the world and shall always
be your loving boy-wife, or your 'little bitch' if you prefer it'.[193]
Neil McKenna states how the term 'bitch was the word in
common usage to indicate a boy who yielded his person to
a lover.'[194] Bosie being a 'bitch' for someone displays that
he could relinquish the power and control he craved, as he
normally took the active role.

Calculated in his approach with Wilde, Bosie had far
more to gain from the relationship, 'sexually, Bosie and

---

190     Croft-Cooke, p. 301.
191     Furneaux.
192     McKenna, p. 187.
193     Liane Jones, 'Bosie's Love Letters Point to Cover-up in Oscar Wilde Trial',
        *The Independent*, 2011 <https://www.independent.co.uk/news/people/
        news/bosies-love-letters-point-to-cover-up-inoscar-wilde-trial-2254136.
        html> [accessed 27 July 2019].
194     McKenna, p. 152.

Wilde were incompatible; each was too dominant by nature to submit to the other'.[195] Lynn Carr states that being passive is 'associated with not being 'wholly masculine'.[196]

'In romantic love we often fall in love with our self, projected onto the other',[197] Bosie wants to be like Wilde, seeing his own talents as comparable. But Bosie's intellectual ability falls short, such as his inability to complete the translation of Wilde's *Salomé*[198] sufficiently. Wilde felt that Bosie's efforts were unacceptable.[199]

Before his trial, Wilde commented how Bosie was more interested in a new brand of champagne recommended to them than the actual trial,[200] displaying his constant lack of awareness. This marked the beginning of the end, the catalyst for the 'decline of [Bosie] into genteel poverty' in later life.[201]

---

195    Robert, p. 155.
196    Lynn Carr and others, 'Same Sex Intimacies: Families of Choice and Other Life Experiments', *Contemporary Sociology*, 31 (2002), 410, p. 146.
197    Minsky, p. 38.
198    Croft-Cooke, p. 60.
199    Ellmann, p. 379.
200    McKenna, p. 352.
201    Gillespie, p. 504.

# Historical context

'Queer history properly considered is the attempt to recover the authentic voice of queer experience rather than simply to document suppression of oppression'.[202] There is an entire life to be considered, an extensive family history, the legality of love.

Born in 1870, Bosie developed a relationship with famous playwright Oscar Wilde when he was twenty-one. The two had met in the summer of 1891,[203] introduced by a mutual friend, Lionel Johnson. Bosie and Lionel were friends at Oxford, Lionel was 'a delightful fellow, though exceedingly eccentric'.[204] During that first meeting, Bosie, Lionel and Wilde exchanged pleasantries.[205] People were enchanted by Bosie's perfect manners,[206] dazzled by his beauty,[207] and Wilde was no exception to this. Wilde arranged to see Bosie a few days later at the Albemarle Club,[208] they quickly became close friends and eventual lovers. They became inseparable. Wilde was so 'enamoured that he essentially abandoned

---

202    Rictor Norton, 'A Critique of Social Constructionism and Postmodern Queer Theory, 'Social Constructionism', *Sourcebook*.
203    Trevor. Fisher, *Oscar and Bosie: A Fatal Passion*, first edition (Stroud: Sutton Pub, 2002), p. 35.
204    Montgomery Hyde, *Lord Alfred Douglas: A Biography* (London: Methuen, 1984), p. 24.
205    Hyde, p. 25.
206    Casper Wintermans, *Alfred Douglas: A Poet's Life and His Finest Work*, first edition (London: Peter Owen Publishers, 2007) p. 31.
207    Neil, McKenna, *The Secret Life of Oscar Wilde* (New York: Basic Books, 2005), p. 300.
208    Hyde, p. 25.

his family to be with [Bosie]'.[209] Aware of how special Wilde found him, Bosie was able to push Wilde to the limits of expectations. In return Wilde 'flaunted [Bosie] at hotels in London and the country'.[210] Wilde diverged from the Victorian norm of masculinity, 'defined by stringency, self-control, self-effacement, and [earnestness]', he had a 'general oddness',[211] that was discomforting to Victorian society, but alluring to Bosie.

However, Bosie's father, the Marquess, didn't approve of this "friendship". He had a 'reputation as being a belligerent, nonconforming aristocrat'[212] and sought to rid Bosie of Wilde by any means necessary. The Marquess started to harass them, so Bosie 'wanted to see his father publicly humiliated';[213] however, it was Wilde who suffered the consequences and humiliation. Through April and May of 1895, Wilde endured three trials at the Old Bailey, the last two defending himself against twenty-five counts of gross indecency. Initially, the Marquess had implied that Wilde looked like a sodomite, 'he refrained, from delicacy or sheer denial, of citing Wilde, and thereby his son, with physical misconduct: "I am not going to try and analyse this intimacy,"

---

209    Rios Jones, p. 64.
210    Freeman's Journal, 'The Oscar Wilde Case', *Freeman's Journal*, 20 August 1895 <http://tinyurl.galegroup.com/tinyurl/BYkok5>.
211    Salamensky, p. 578.
212    David Schulz, 'Redressing Oscar: Performance and the Trials of Oscar Wilde', *TDR (1988–)*, 40.2 (1996), 37–59, p. 39.
213    Rios Jones, p. 64.

the Marquess wrote Bosie'.[214] In essence, the Marquess had only accused Wilde of posing as a homosexual, not of being one. Wilde was 'urged on by the rebellious Bosie and confused solicitor' to file a libel suit against the Marquess.[215]

Telling the story of a historical character has challenges, including misremembered reports and incorrect accounts. One example of this is newspaper reports on an altercation between Bosie and his father in May 1895. In one newspaper, it was reported that Bosie exclaimed to his father 'you have threatened me; now carry out your threat. You are a liar and a slanderer,' a large crowd supposedly formed and the Marquess replied to his son, 'I tell all these strangers that you have been a bad son, from your birth, and that I now publicly disown you'. The two then began a physical fight, the police arrived and, with great difficulty, separated the two. Bosie had discoloration to one eye, and the Marquess' silk hat 'showed signs of rather rough usage'.[216] The report was sensationalised; the fight didn't involve Bosie, but was actually between his brother, Percy, and their father, the Marquess.[217] This reinforces the fact that the public had been whipped into a frenzy by the press, who were trying to

214     Salamensky, p. 577.
215     Salamensky, p. 576.
216     'Multiple News Items', *The Standard*, 19 August 1895, p. 3 <http://tinyurl. galegroup.com/tinyurl/BYYup4>, p. 3.
217     Illustrated Police News, '"The Queensberry Case": Newspaper Coverage of the Queensberry Trial', 1 June 1895.

outdo each other with shocking and distasteful stories.[218] Other accounts of the same quarrel explained how '[Percy] was reduced to the absolute necessity of adopting the course he did, of publicly assaulting [the Marquess]'.[219] It is important to note that Wilde was an exploiter of media attention and was a well-known commodity to the press, previously enjoying publicity and the press, having a hunger for fame and success, parlaying 'the growing technology of newspaper reproduction and distribution to enhance his celebrity persona'.[220]

*The Picture of Dorian Gray*, for example, published in July 1890, had initial critical backlash, but 'Wilde was courting this controversy, harnessing it to increase his fame'.[221] During the libel trial, Wilde had two successful plays running in the West End. The plays were society comedies that 'propelled him to fame and fortune, setting the stage for his tragic and sudden fall from grace.'[222] The Marquess's lawyer, Edward Carson, spoke about *The Picture of Dorian Gray*, describing the novel as containing 'relations, intimacies and passions of certain persons of sodomitical and unnatural habits, tastes

218  Murray, p. 86.
219  'Trial of Oscar Wilde', *Aberdeen Journal* (Aberdeen, 27 May 1895) http://tinyurl.galegroup.com/tinyurl/BYkyM4.
220  Schulz, p. 40.
221  Rios Jones, and Pedro Daniel, ‹Oscar Wilde the prisoner, and the carceral›, *Atenea*, 33. 1-2 (January-December 2013), p. 57.
222  Rios Jones, p. 58.

and practices'.[223] To the jury, *Dorian Gray* was proof of Wilde's homosexuality.[224] Also used in court was Bosie's poem 'Two Loves'[225], in which the homoerotic character states, 'I am the love that dare not speak its name'.[226] Despite this, Bosie found himself omitted from implications of illegal activity, protected by both his father and his lover. But it was Wilde who became forced 'to defend himself, his wife, and his sons from what could be ruinous rumours? To revenge himself on the irksome Marquess, thus securing his son's fickle affections? To stage another sold-out show, rendering the court room of theatre? It is, indeed, unclear from Wilde's tactics whether he wishes to challenge the court's approval or flout its rule, challenge Queensberry's characterisation of him, or prove its acceptability.'[227] 'Wilde technically sought action against a claim of seeming different [...] The introduction of material evidence by [the Marquess'] defence upped the ante from issues of posing to being, from civil difference to criminal difference'.[228] The Marquess garnered an array of witnesses, paying them handsomely for their testimony. The Marquess had offered the renters 'inflated

---

223    Merlin Holland, *The Real Trial of Oscar Wilde: With an Introduction and Commentary*, first edition (New York: Perennial, 2004), p. 39.
224    Patrick Mason, 'Acting Out', *Irish University Review*, 32.1 (2002), 137–47, p. 139.
225    Murray, p. 55.
226    Holland, p. 68.
227    Salamensky, p. 580.
228    Salamensky, p. 581.

fees to say what they were told to say and [made] threats of prosecution should they choose to do otherwise'.[229] Those renters had partaken in homosexual activity, admitted to it, and provided testimony about it, were not found guilty themselves or have charges brought about against them. Erving Goffman states how, 'the successful blackmailer, in addition to the blackmail, also avoids the penalty attached to blackmailing'.[230] Their crimes 'remained inadmissible because their word supported the prosecution's charges against Wilde'.[231]

By the end of the first trial, the libel case against the Marquess, the jury had agreed that the Marquess was 'not guilty' of libel and the defence stated how the evidence surrounding Wilde would result in 'an investigation of matters of the most appalling character'.[232] The trials had 'brought to an end Wilde's fame and prosperity'.[233]

Wilde's wife, Constance, vacated Tite Street, removed their sons from school and became dependent upon her cousin who despised Wilde. Her cousin tried tirelessly to drive a wedge further between Constance and Wilde, referring to him as 'the beast'.[234] Constance's friends and

---

229    Bristow, p. 42.
230    Goffman, p. 97.
231    Bristow, p. 42
232    Holland, p. 281.
233    Rios Jones, p. 57.
234    Fido, p. 113.

family encouraged her to petition for a divorce; instead, she changed her name to Holland. Similar to Bosie, she then fled to the continent in order to avoid the media hysteria. However, in 1896, she returned to London from Genoa to visit Wilde in prison, sharing the news of his mother's passing, the two also discussed the future.[235] Constance, who had once admired Bosie, now referred to him as a 'beast' and she still couldn't comprehend homosexuality and Wilde's desire.[236]

## Similar trials

Several cases from this time involving homosexuals are invaluable in understanding the differences in and in reporting. There were, and still are, 'difficulties experienced by gay men in a hostile society',[237] Bosie and Wilde were no exception to this. Looking at the treatment of homosexuals throughout history, homosexuality was viewed as sexual deviation, 'in the fourteenth – and fifteenth century [...] men found in suspicious circumstances were presumed guilty',[238] this 'presumed' guilt extended to 1895 and beyond, as Wilde stood on trial. Wilde received two years hard labour, whereas his homosexual predecessors of the Middle Ages

---

235    Fido, p. 125.
236    Fido, p. 130.
237    Michael King and Annie Bartlett, 'British Psychiatry and Homosexuality', The British Journal of Psychiatry: The Journal of Mental Science, 175 (1999), 106–13, p. 109.
238    Rictor Norton, *A History of Homophobia*, <http://rictornorton.co.uk/homophob.htm>

would have been burnt at the stake.[239] Some men who were caught engaging in homosexual activities would simply kill themselves after their arrest.[240]

Past trials involving gross indecency and libel establish a history of the crime itself and subsequent punishment. This comparison shows the prosecution's aim to bring down Wilde by any means necessary. Examining the Keevil Libel Case of 1879,[241] in which the vicar of Keevil, Reverend William Henry Chamberlain, brought libel charges against a fellow clergyman for writing that he'd partaken in acts of sodomy and acts of depravity with both young girls and young men. A vast array of witnesses came forward to give evidence to prove the accusations. A young woman claimed she'd been detained by the vicar in a shrubbery when she was fifteen; a young man of sixteen witnessed the vicar commit unnatural offences; numerous young men were also seen to enter a shed with the vicar; and in the evenings young men would meander the 'vicarage grounds wandering among the shrubs'. The judge stated that 'the libels are of the most serious nature [...] they impute a man of advanced years, a minister of religion, [...] they impute to him unnatural and foul gratifications with young men. I cannot conceive a graver

---

239    Norton, p. 2.
240    Norton, p. 4.
241    Norton, 'The Keevil Libel Case, 1879', *Homosexuality in Nineteenth-Century England: A Sourcebook*.

charge'. But, after only seventy minutes deliberation, the jury returned with a verdict in favour of the vicar, awarding damages of £50 for the harm done to his character.[242] The vicar won his libel case despite the abundance of evidence. Continuing to serve as the vicar of Keevil for over sixty years, becoming one of the oldest clergymen in England, dying at the age of ninety-two.

Additionally, the case of the Hulme Fancy Dress Ball in 1880.[243, 244] On 27th September 1880, a raid took place at the Temperance Hall in Hulme, Manchester, resulting in the arrest of forty-seven men. Men had arrived at the ball in female attire, with one man dressed as Juliet. Newspapers reported that all men present 'were charged with soliciting and inciting each other to commit sodomy, and with conspiring to assemble for that purpose. Evidence of gross indecencies was given by the police.'[245] The men's ages ranged from eighteen to forty-eight, they had varying professions, such as schoolmaster, bookkeeper, draper, painter, grocer, chemist and mechanic, and some of the men had wives and children. It was quantified that these men partook in 'odious

242    Rictor Norton, 'The Keevil Libel Case, 1879', Homosexuality in Nineteenth-
       Century England: A Sourcebook.
243    Harry Cocks, Nameless Offences: Homosexual Desire in the Nineteenth
       Century, first edition (London: I.B. Tauris, 2003), p. 70-71.
244    Matt Cook, A Gay History of Britain: Love and Sex between Men since the
       Middle Ages, first edition (Oxford: Greenwood world Publishing, 2007), p.
       118.
245    Rictor Norton, 'Hulme Fancy Dress Ball, 1880', Homosexuality in
       Nineteenth-Century England: A Sourcebook.

practices' and that was a 'vice – a vice so hateful that it was unnameable among Christians'. Despite the evidence and serious charges, the forty-seven men received only a fine of £25 each, and 'to be of good behaviour for twelve months, or in default, three months' imprisonment'.[246] This occurred in 1880, five years before Wilde was tried and charged with two-years hard labour, displaying the court's desire to make a spectacle out of Wilde and stamp out this 'odious' issue of homosexuality.

A final case, from Wilde's home country, took place only a year before his own, the Dublin Scandals of 1884.[247] A multi-faceted case involving men of varying stations, resulting in many arrests from accusations of the foulest offences.[248] It resulted in a libel case where evidence was provided on the indecent acts, including sodomy. Sexual partners were found from friendship networks, arrests were made, charges brought about for sodomy and for 'procuring [others] to commit sodomy'.[249] Fearful the government may be portrayed as 'lacking in heterosexual mainlines',[250] witnesses were arrested, warrants issued and police were actively engaged. The results

---

246    Norton, 'Hulme Fancy Dress Ball, 1880'.
247    Cocks, p. 140.
248    Daniel Monk, 'Aleardo Zanghellini, The Sexual Constitution of Political Authority: The "Trials" of Same-Sex Desire', *Sexualities*, 19.8 (2016), 1003–8, p. 131.
249    Rictor Norton (Ed.), 'The Dublin Scandals, 1884', *Homosexuality in Nineteenth-Century England: A Sourcebook*, p. 44.
250    Monk, p. 136.

of the trials led to some men being sentenced to two years' hard labour, with some having their sanity questioned and others receiving acquittals.[251]

These three trials build to a crescendo of Wilde's untimely demise, each becoming gradually worse for the accused. First, a vicar who won; then forty-seven men who each received a £25 fine, and finally a case which resulted in a vast array of outcomes for all involved. These cases expand the understanding of the social attitudes of the time, along with the Crown's view of homosexuality. In Bosie's own words, he declared that the Crown, representing the country, is to blame for what happened to Wilde: 'let England bear the responsibility for what she did to [Wilde]'.[252]

## Regina v. Wilde

Rumours and gossip about Bosie and Wilde were reaching the Marquess.[253] In retaliation, he chastised them publicly and sent Bosie letters with obscene requests and demands. The Marquess made plans to disrupt Wilde's play, *The Importance of Being Earnest*, but Wilde ensured that the Marquess wouldn't be admitted to the theatre. The Marquess then ventured to the Albemarle Club, where he left a calling card, endorsed 'To Oscar Wilde posing as a somdomite'.

---

251    Rictor Norton (Ed.), 'The Dublin Scandals, 1884', *Homosexuality in Nineteenth-Century England: A Sourcebook*, p. 1.
252    Stokes and Stokes, p. 12.
253    Fido, p. 104.

The libel trial against the Marquess lasted only three days,[254] due to the monumental efforts of the Marquess and his defence team in gathering evidence presented to the court proving Wilde's homosexuality. When Wilde left the courtroom and 'the DPP, the Home Secretary and the Solicitor-General agreed that Wilde should be taken into custody',[255] he was charged, held without bail and forced to spend almost three weeks in Holloway Prison. Two further trials then took place, 'with Wilde as defendant against the state's charges of "indecency" with men'.[256]

Wilde wasn't the first man to be blackmailed by renters; many men in London during this time would become entrapped in 'cruising grounds such as Piccadilly. Once entrapped, the client was subjected to threats, intimidation, and even physical violence'.[257] Both Bosie and Wilde had been blackmailed before, sensitive letters had fallen into a renter's hands.[258] The renter would extort money from Wilde for love letters written to Bosie.[259] The jury were told to condemn Wilde's homosexual behaviours, but not the renters... that the blackmail had only occurred as result of the sodomy

---

254     Schulz, p. 39.
255     Bristow, p.44.
256     Salamensky, p. 582.
257     Bristow, p. 43.
258     Holland, p. 31.
259     'Trial of Oscar Wilde', *Aberdeen Journal* (Aberdeen, 27 May 1895) <http://tinyurl.galegroup.com/tinyurl/BYkyM4>.

Wilde had inflicted upon them.[260] The prosecution urged the jury to 'observe the oath' that the renters had taken,[261] alluding that no one would lie under oath. After deliberating, the jury couldn't reach a verdict and so Wilde was released on bail for three weeks.

During Wilde's second criminal trial, the foreman of the jury asked the judge if a guilty verdict against Wilde would 'affect Lord Alfred Douglas', the judge stated that 'the continued intimacy was as damaging to the reputation of the recipient as to the sender, but that had nothing to do with the present inquiry'.[262] Bosie had escaped judgement and charges, 'since [Bosie] was not called during the libel trial and remained on the continent during the two criminal trials that followed, it was left to Wilde to withstand alone the often humiliating cross-examination'.[263]

The prosecution ignored the fact that the young men whom Wilde had 'sexually exploited' were then 'understandably tempted by the prospect of blackmail'.[264] Solicitor-General Frank Lockwood, the lead prosecutor, urged the jury to see the young men, the renters, who testified against Wilde and who had once blackmailed Wilde, as

---

260    Bristow, p. 46.
261    Freeman's Journal, 'The Oscar Wilde Case', *Freeman's Journal*, 20 August 1895 <http://tinyurl.galegroup.com/tinyurl/BYkok5>.
262    York Herald, p. 5.
263    Bristow, p. 45.
264    Bristow, p. 46.

individuals who would see their own reputation suffer from doing so; this was actually the case for some, for instance, Charles Oliver Parker, a former renter who had found a place within the Royal Artillery, was discharged only a few days after the end of the third trial, being told that his 'services were no longer required'.[265] Charles Gill, the prosecutor in the first criminal trial said that Bosie was a victim of Wilde and that the Marquess was only taking necessary action to protect his son, and that any father would do the same. Gill continued, 'Douglas, if guilty, may fairly be regarded as one of Wilde's victims' and that it would be challenging to find evidence to 'prove anything definite' surrounding Bosie and Wilde's 'immoral relations'.[266] The court was horrified hearing how Wilde bought young men 'luxurious dinners, extravagant gifts or expensive clothes'.[267]

Wilde had solicited and incited Maurice Schwabe to 'commit sodomy and other acts of gross indecency and immorality'.[268] At that time, Schwabe's identity was concealed, due to him being the defence's nephew-in-law. Schwabe had been instructed to leave the country ahead of the trials,[269] thereby eradicating any implication. Schwabe

---

265   Holland, p. 318.
266   Holland, p. 294.
267   Schulz, p. 50.
268   Holland, p. 288.
269   Ellmann, p. 430.

was merely referred to as being 'another gentleman'.[270] Similar to Bosie, Schwabe was protected by his family. There was hypocrisy surrounding witnesses, the renters, who themselves were admitting to blackmailing men.[271] Some witnesses received £20 from the Marquess, the equivalent of a year's salary, while others received £5 a week, confirming that it was 'more bribery than expenses'.[272]

During the trial, Bosie's tantrums and temper were exposed to the court, a letter from Wilde to Bosie was read aloud and sections printed in newspapers, 'you must not make scenes with me. They kill me. They wreck the loveliness of life. I cannot listen to your curved lips saying hideous things to me. Do not do it, you break my heart'.[273] The court stated that Bosie, 'if guilty, would not be spared because he was Lord Alfred Douglas',[274] his title and status wouldn't have saved him. The newspapers reported that 'Lord Alfred Douglas was now in Paris, where he went at [Wilde's] desire'.[275] Another letter used in court, from Wilde to Bosie, referred to Bosie's 'roseleaf lips', and the 'madness

270    Holland, p. 161.
271    Bristow, 56.
272    Holland, p. xxxvii.
273    'Trial of Oscar Wilde', *Aberdeen Journal* (Aberdeen, 27 May 1895) <http://tinyurl.galegroup.com/tinyurl/BYkyM4>.
274    Freeman's Journal, 'THE OSCAR WILDE CASE', *Freeman's Journal*, 20 August 1895 <http://tinyurl.galegroup.com/tinyurl/BYkok5>.
275    'Trial of Oscar Wilde', *Aberdeen Journal* (Aberdeen, 27 May 1895) <http://tinyurl.galegroup.com/tinyurl/BYkyM4>.

of kissing'.[276] The jury felt that this letter 'pointed to unclean relations' questioning if the contents were 'for purposes of charity or for wicked purposes'.[277]

The Marquess's 'attorneys went to such unprincipled lengths [...] in order to strengthen his plea of justification that Wilde was a sodomite',[278] the prosecution pushed the notion that Wilde's homosexual activities were far worse than blackmail. Wilde was a wealthy homosexual that 'exploited susceptible young men'.[279] The only people admitting to a crime were testifying for the prosecution.[280] During sentencing the jury found Wilde guilty.[281] The judge stated 'this was a painful and shocking case, [...] he would rather try a most shocking murder case than be engaged in trying one of these cases', Wilde sat in the dock, displaying signs of 'considerable anxiety'.[282]

The judge stated in conclusion that 'the jury had arrived at the correct verdict [...] People who can do these things must be dead to all sense of shame, and one cannot hope to produce any effect on them. [...] that you, Wilde, have been

---

276  'Oscar Wilde's Trial', *Blackburn Standard*, 20 August 1895, p. 2 <http://tinyurl.galegroup.com/tinyurl/BYkwXX>.
277  Freeman's Journal, 'The Oscar Wilde Case', *Freeman's Journal*, 20 August 1895 <http://tinyurl.galegroup.com/tinyurl/BYkok5>.
278  Bristow, p. 49.
279  Bristow, p. 49.
280  Bristow, p, 50.
281  'Oscar Wildes Trial', *Blackburn Standard*, 20 August 1895, p. 2 <http://tinyurl.galegroup.com/tinyurl/BYkwXX>.
282  Herald, p. 5.

the centre of a circle of extensive corruption of the most hideous kind among young men, it is equally impossible to doubt. I shall, under the circumstances, be expected to pass the severest sentence that the law allows. In my judgement it is totally inadequate for such a case as this.'[283]

The press reported that Wilde 'seemed quite dazed, stood with fixed gaze and trembling hands, and looked as if about to faint [...] Wilde held up his hands as if to keep them off, and addressed the court in a few unintelligible words, he was then hurried below'.[284] Society had enjoyed the scandal and entertainment of Wilde and the trials but this diminished, turning to cruelty and venom after his conviction. The name 'Oscar' fell into almost total disuse, and Wilde's name was removed from posters and programmes, his published work also removed from shops, there was a general consensus that 'a disgraced man must not be allowed a living'.[285] Bosie had been 'illuminated in a blaze of reflected glory' by Oscar's success.[286] In the last moments of the play, the character confides, melancholic to the audience, that he will be nothing more than 'Oscar's boy Bosie'.[287]

---

283    Bristow, p. 51.
284    'Trial of Oscar Wilde', *Aberdeen Journal* (Aberdeen, 27 May 1895) <http://tinyurl.galegroup.com/tinyurl/BYkyM4>.
285    Fido, p. 117.
286    Fisher, p. 61.
287    Barnett, Act Two, p ?.

## Acknowledgements

Thanks to Peter Collins at Polari Plays, the wonderful team at Greater Manchester Fringe Festival, my director Tuirenn Hurstfield and especially my parents for always supporting and encouraging my passion.

## Polari Press

Taking our name from the secret slang Polari, we are an independent publishing house that seeks out hidden voices and helps them be heard.

Although Polari was spoken almost exclusively by gay and bisexual men, the nature of clandestine meetings of the mid-1900s, when homosexuality was still criminalised, brought together people from all walks of life who all had an influence on the language.

Cockney, Romany, and Italian languages mixed with the colloquialisms of thespians, circus performers, wrestlers, sailors, and wider criminal communities to create a slang to express their sexuality secretly and safely.

Inspired by these origins, we publish queer voices as well as other marginalised groups, to share our perspectives with each other and help build a collaborative platform for all of us.

polari.com

## Polari Plays

We are creating an active archive for queer-authored play scripts and performance.

For a complete listing of Polari Plays titles, visit:
`polari.press/plays`

Follow us on social media:
`@PolariPress`